C-297 CAREER EXAMINATION SERIES

This is your PASSBOOK for...

Gardener

Test Preparation Study Guide
Questions & Answers

NLC®
NATIONAL LEARNING CORPORATION®

National Learning Corporation

212 Michael Drive, Syosset, NY 11791
(516) 921-8888 • www.passbooks.com
E-mail: info@passbooks.com

PASSBOOK® SERIES

THE *PASSBOOK® SERIES* has been created to prepare applicants and candidates for the ultimate academic battlefield – the examination room.

At some time in our lives, each and every one of us may be required to take an examination – for validation, matriculation, admission, qualification, registration, certification, or licensure.

Based on the assumption that every applicant or candidate has met the basic formal educational standards, has taken the required number of courses, and read the necessary texts, the *PASSBOOK® SERIES* furnishes the one special preparation which may assure passing with confidence, instead of failing with insecurity. Examination questions – together with answers – are furnished as the basic vehicle for study so that the mysteries of the examination and its compounding difficulties may be eliminated or diminished by a sure method.

This book is meant to help you pass your examination provided that you qualify and are serious in your objective.

The entire field is reviewed through the huge store of content information which is succinctly presented through a provocative and challenging approach – the question-and-answer method.

A climate of success is established by furnishing the correct answers at the end of each test.

You soon learn to recognize types of questions, forms of questions, and patterns of questioning. You may even begin to anticipate expected outcomes.

You perceive that many questions are repeated or adapted so that you can gain acute insights, which may enable you to score many sure points.

You learn how to confront new questions, or types of questions, and to attack them confidently and work out the correct answers.

You note objectives and emphases, and recognize pitfalls and dangers, so that you may make positive educational adjustments.

Moreover, you are kept fully informed in relation to new concepts, methods, practices, and directions in the field.

You discover that you are actually taking the examination all the time: you are preparing for the examination by "taking" an examination, not by reading extraneous and/or supererogatory textbooks.

In short, this PASSBOOK®, used directedly, should be an important factor in helping you to pass your test.

GARDENER

DUTIES

Gardeners, under supervision, assist in and perform tasks such as site preparation, planting, cultivating, and caring for trees, flowers, plants, shrubs, lawns and other flora; assist in and perform tasks involved in the operation and maintenance of hand and power gardening tools and equipment; perform simple record keeping and prepare simple written reports; drive vehicles and operate other motorized equipment in the performance of duties. All Gardeners perform related work. Gardeners may supervise subordinate employees, including temporary workers, instructing them in gardening techniques and in the proper use and care of materials and equipment. Gardeners are required to drive motor vehicles to and from work sites and to transport plants and materials.

EXAMPLES OF TYPICAL TASKS

Plants, cultivates, and cares for trees, flowers, plants, shrubs, and other flora. Digs up, balls, burlaps, and transplants trees and shrubs. Digs up and transplants sod. Pots flowers and plants. Propagates plant life. Prepares soil and seed beds. Grades, sods, weeds, mulches, and mows lawns. Repairs damaged planted areas. As necessary, fertilizes and waters soil, prunes and sprays trees, shrubs, and plants. Operates and cares for hand and power gardening tools and equipment and makes necessary operating adjustments to same; reports need for repairs and replacements. As required, keeps simple records and makes written reports. As directed, performs various tasks in connection with cleaning of grounds and painting of fixtures and equipment.

SCOPE OF THE EXAMINATION

The multiple-choice test may include questions on turf establishment and management; cultivation, propagation, planting, pruning and identification of trees, shrubs, flowers, and other plant materials; operation and maintenance of hand and mechanized gardening tools; handling and use of pesticides, herbicides, fertilizers, lime and soil conditioners; diagnosis and treatment of plant diseases and insect infestation; basic botany and plant physiology; and other related areas. The test may also include questions requiring the use of deductive reasoning, inductive reasoning, information ordering, number facility, problem sensitivity, visualization, and written expression.

HOW TO TAKE A TEST

I. YOU MUST PASS AN EXAMINATION

A. WHAT EVERY CANDIDATE SHOULD KNOW

Examination applicants often ask us for help in preparing for the written test. What can I study in advance? What kinds of questions will be asked? How will the test be given? How will the papers be graded?

As an applicant for a civil service examination, you may be wondering about some of these things. Our purpose here is to suggest effective methods of advance study and to describe civil service examinations.

Your chances for success on this examination can be increased if you know how to prepare. Those "pre-examination jitters" can be reduced if you know what to expect. You can even experience an adventure in good citizenship if you know why civil service exams are given.

B. WHY ARE CIVIL SERVICE EXAMINATIONS GIVEN?

Civil service examinations are important to you in two ways. As a citizen, you want public jobs filled by employees who know how to do their work. As a job seeker, you want a fair chance to compete for that job on an equal footing with other candidates. The best-known means of accomplishing this two-fold goal is the competitive examination.

Exams are widely publicized throughout the nation. They may be administered for jobs in federal, state, city, municipal, town or village governments or agencies.

Any citizen may apply, with some limitations, such as the age or residence of applicants. Your experience and education may be reviewed to see whether you meet the requirements for the particular examination. When these requirements exist, they are reasonable and applied consistently to all applicants. Thus, a competitive examination may cause you some uneasiness now, but it is your privilege and safeguard.

C. HOW ARE CIVIL SERVICE EXAMS DEVELOPED?

Examinations are carefully written by trained technicians who are specialists in the field known as "psychological measurement," in consultation with recognized authorities in the field of work that the test will cover. These experts recommend the subject matter areas or skills to be tested; only those knowledges or skills important to your success on the job are included. The most reliable books and source materials available are used as references. Together, the experts and technicians judge the difficulty level of the questions.

Test technicians know how to phrase questions so that the problem is clearly stated. Their ethics do not permit "trick" or "catch" questions. Questions may have been tried out on sample groups, or subjected to statistical analysis, to determine their usefulness.

Written tests are often used in combination with performance tests, ratings of training and experience, and oral interviews. All of these measures combine to form the best-known means of finding the right person for the right job.

II. HOW TO PASS THE WRITTEN TEST

A. NATURE OF THE EXAMINATION

To prepare intelligently for civil service examinations, you should know how they differ from school examinations you have taken. In school you were assigned certain definite pages to read or subjects to cover. The examination questions were quite detailed and usually emphasized memory. Civil service exams, on the other hand, try to discover your present ability to perform the duties of a position, plus your potentiality to learn these duties. In other words, a civil service exam attempts to predict how successful you will be. Questions cover such a broad area that they cannot be as minute and detailed as school exam questions.

In the public service similar kinds of work, or positions, are grouped together in one "class." This process is known as *position-classification.* All the positions in a class are paid according to the salary range for that class. One class title covers all of these positions, and they are all tested by the same examination.

B. FOUR BASIC STEPS

1) Study the announcement

How, then, can you know what subjects to study? Our best answer is: "Learn as much as possible about the class of positions for which you've applied." The exam will test the knowledge, skills and abilities needed to do the work.

Your most valuable source of information about the position you want is the official exam announcement. This announcement lists the training and experience qualifications. Check these standards and apply only if you come reasonably close to meeting them.

The brief description of the position in the examination announcement offers some clues to the subjects which will be tested. Think about the job itself. Review the duties in your mind. Can you perform them, or are there some in which you are rusty? Fill in the blank spots in your preparation.

Many jurisdictions preview the written test in the exam announcement by including a section called "Knowledge and Abilities Required," "Scope of the Examination," or some similar heading. Here you will find out specifically what fields will be tested.

2) Review your own background

Once you learn in general what the position is all about, and what you need to know to do the work, ask yourself which subjects you already know fairly well and which need improvement. You may wonder whether to concentrate on improving your strong areas or on building some background in your fields of weakness. When the announcement has specified "some knowledge" or "considerable knowledge," or has used adjectives like "beginning principles of..." or "advanced ... methods," you can get a clue as to the number and difficulty of questions to be asked in any given field. More questions, and hence broader coverage, would be included for those subjects which are more important in the work. Now weigh your strengths and weaknesses against the job requirements and prepare accordingly.

3) Determine the level of the position

Another way to tell how intensively you should prepare is to understand the level of the job for which you are applying. Is it the entering level? In other words, is this the position in which beginners in a field of work are hired? Or is it an intermediate or advanced level? Sometimes this is indicated by such words as "Junior" or "Senior" in the class title. Other jurisdictions use Roman numerals to designate the level – Clerk I, Clerk II, for example. The word "Supervisor" sometimes appears in the title. If the level is not indicated by the title, check the description of duties. Will you be working under very close supervision, or will you have responsibility for independent decisions in this work?

4) Choose appropriate study materials

Now that you know the subjects to be examined and the relative amount of each subject to be covered, you can choose suitable study materials. For beginning level jobs, or even advanced ones, if you have a pronounced weakness in some aspect of your training, read a modern, standard textbook in that field. Be sure it is up to date and has general coverage. Such books are normally available at your library, and the librarian will be glad to help you locate one. For entry-level positions, questions of appropriate difficulty are chosen – neither highly advanced questions, nor those too simple. Such questions require careful thought but not advanced training.

If the position for which you are applying is technical or advanced, you will read more advanced, specialized material. If you are already familiar with the basic principles of your field, elementary textbooks would waste your time. Concentrate on advanced textbooks and technical periodicals. Think through the concepts and review difficult problems in your field.

These are all general sources. You can get more ideas on your own initiative, following these leads. For example, training manuals and publications of the government agency which employs workers in your field can be useful, particularly for technical and professional positions. A letter or visit to the government department involved may result in more specific study suggestions, and certainly will provide you with a more definite idea of the exact nature of the position you are seeking.

III. KINDS OF TESTS

Tests are used for purposes other than measuring knowledge and ability to perform specified duties. For some positions, it is equally important to test ability to make adjustments to new situations or to profit from training. In others, basic mental abilities not dependent on information are essential. Questions which test these things may not appear as pertinent to the duties of the position as those which test for knowledge and information. Yet they are often highly important parts of a fair examination. For very general questions, it is almost impossible to help you direct your study efforts. What we can do is to point out some of the more common of these general abilities needed in public service positions and describe some typical questions.

1) General information

Broad, general information has been found useful for predicting job success in some kinds of work. This is tested in a variety of ways, from vocabulary lists to questions about current events. Basic background in some field of work, such as sociology or economics, may be sampled in a group of questions. Often these are principles which have become familiar to most persons through exposure rather than through formal training. It is difficult to advise you how to study for these questions; being alert to the world around you is our best suggestion.

2) Verbal ability

An example of an ability needed in many positions is verbal or language ability. Verbal ability is, in brief, the ability to use and understand words. Vocabulary and grammar tests are typical measures of this ability. Reading comprehension or paragraph interpretation questions are common in many kinds of civil service tests. You are given a paragraph of written material and asked to find its central meaning.

3) Numerical ability

Number skills can be tested by the familiar arithmetic problem, by checking paired lists of numbers to see which are alike and which are different, or by interpreting charts and graphs. In the latter test, a graph may be printed in the test booklet which you are asked to use as the basis for answering questions.

4) Observation

A popular test for law-enforcement positions is the observation test. A picture is shown to you for several minutes, then taken away. Questions about the picture test your ability to observe both details and larger elements.

5) Following directions

In many positions in the public service, the employee must be able to carry out written instructions dependably and accurately. You may be given a chart with several columns, each column listing a variety of information. The questions require you to carry out directions involving the information given in the chart.

6) Skills and aptitudes

Performance tests effectively measure some manual skills and aptitudes. When the skill is one in which you are trained, such as typing or shorthand, you can practice. These tests are often very much like those given in business school or high school courses. For many of the other skills and aptitudes, however, no short-time preparation can be made. Skills and abilities natural to you or that you have developed throughout your lifetime are being tested.

Many of the general questions just described provide all the data needed to answer the questions and ask you to use your reasoning ability to find the answers. Your best preparation for these tests, as well as for tests of facts and ideas, is to be at your physical and mental best. You, no doubt, have your own methods of getting into an exam-taking mood and keeping "in shape." The next section lists some ideas on this subject.

IV. KINDS OF QUESTIONS

Only rarely is the "essay" question, which you answer in narrative form, used in civil service tests. Civil service tests are usually of the short-answer type. Full instructions for answering these questions will be given to you at the examination. But in case this is your first experience with short-answer questions and separate answer sheets, here is what you need to know:

1) Multiple-choice Questions

Most popular of the short-answer questions is the "multiple choice" or "best answer" question. It can be used, for example, to test for factual knowledge, ability to solve problems or judgment in meeting situations found at work.

A multiple-choice question is normally one of three types—

- It can begin with an incomplete statement followed by several possible endings. You are to find the one ending which *best* completes the statement, although some of the others may not be entirely wrong.
- It can also be a complete statement in the form of a question which is answered by choosing one of the statements listed.

- It can be in the form of a problem – again you select the best answer.

Here is an example of a multiple-choice question with a discussion which should give you some clues as to the method for choosing the right answer:

When an employee has a complaint about his assignment, the action which will *best* help him overcome his difficulty is to

A. discuss his difficulty with his coworkers
B. take the problem to the head of the organization
C. take the problem to the person who gave him the assignment
D. say nothing to anyone about his complaint

In answering this question, you should study each of the choices to find which is best. Consider choice "A" – Certainly an employee may discuss his complaint with fellow employees, but no change or improvement can result, and the complaint remains unresolved. Choice "B" is a poor choice since the head of the organization probably does not know what assignment you have been given, and taking your problem to him is known as "going over the head" of the supervisor. The supervisor, or person who made the assignment, is the person who can clarify it or correct any injustice. Choice "C" is, therefore, correct. To say nothing, as in choice "D," is unwise. Supervisors have and interest in knowing the problems employees are facing, and the employee is seeking a solution to his problem.

2) True/False Questions

The "true/false" or "right/wrong" form of question is sometimes used. Here a complete statement is given. Your job is to decide whether the statement is right or wrong.

SAMPLE: A roaming cell-phone call to a nearby city costs less than a non-roaming call to a distant city.

This statement is wrong, or false, since roaming calls are more expensive.

This is not a complete list of all possible question forms, although most of the others are variations of these common types. You will always get complete directions for answering questions. Be sure you understand *how* to mark your answers – ask questions until you do.

V. RECORDING YOUR ANSWERS

Computer terminals are used more and more today for many different kinds of exams.

For an examination with very few applicants, you may be told to record your answers in the test booklet itself. Separate answer sheets are much more common. If this separate answer sheet is to be scored by machine – and this is often the case – it is highly important that you mark your answers correctly in order to get credit.

An electronic scoring machine is often used in civil service offices because of the speed with which papers can be scored. Machine-scored answer sheets must be marked with a pencil, which will be given to you. This pencil has a high graphite content which responds to the electronic scoring machine. As a matter of fact, stray dots may register as answers, so do not let your pencil rest on the answer sheet while you are pondering the correct answer. Also, if your pencil lead breaks or is otherwise defective, ask for another.

Since the answer sheet will be dropped in a slot in the scoring machine, be careful not to bend the corners or get the paper crumpled.

The answer sheet normally has five vertical columns of numbers, with 30 numbers to a column. These numbers correspond to the question numbers in your test booklet. After each number, going across the page are four or five pairs of dotted lines. These short dotted lines have small letters or numbers above them. The first two pairs may also have a "T" or "F" above the letters. This indicates that the first two pairs only are to be used if the questions are of the true-false type. If the questions are multiple choice, disregard the "T" and "F" and pay attention only to the small letters or numbers.

Answer your questions in the manner of the sample that follows:

32. The largest city in the United States is
    A. Washington, D.C.
    B. New York City
    C. Chicago
    D. Detroit
    E. San Francisco

1) Choose the answer you think is best. (New York City is the largest, so "B" is correct.)
2) Find the row of dotted lines numbered the same as the question you are answering. (Find row number 32)
3) Find the pair of dotted lines corresponding to the answer. (Find the pair of lines under the mark "B.")
4) Make a solid black mark between the dotted lines.

VI. BEFORE THE TEST

Common sense will help you find procedures to follow to get ready for an examination. Too many of us, however, overlook these sensible measures. Indeed, nervousness and fatigue have been found to be the most serious reasons why applicants fail to do their best on civil service tests. Here is a list of reminders:

- Begin your preparation early – Don't wait until the last minute to go scurrying around for books and materials or to find out what the position is all about.
- Prepare continuously – An hour a night for a week is better than an all-night cram session. This has been definitely established. What is more, a night a week for a month will return better dividends than crowding your study into a shorter period of time.
- Locate the place of the exam – You have been sent a notice telling you when and where to report for the examination. If the location is in a different town or otherwise unfamiliar to you, it would be well to inquire the best route and learn something about the building.
- Relax the night before the test – Allow your mind to rest. Do not study at all that night. Plan some mild recreation or diversion; then go to bed early and get a good night's sleep.
- Get up early enough to make a leisurely trip to the place for the test – This way unforeseen events, traffic snarls, unfamiliar buildings, etc. will not upset you.
- Dress comfortably – A written test is not a fashion show. You will be known by number and not by name, so wear something comfortable.

- Leave excess paraphernalia at home – Shopping bags and odd bundles will get in your way. You need bring only the items mentioned in the official notice you received; usually everything you need is provided. Do not bring reference books to the exam. They will only confuse those last minutes and be taken away from you when in the test room.
- Arrive somewhat ahead of time – If because of transportation schedules you must get there very early, bring a newspaper or magazine to take your mind off yourself while waiting.
- Locate the examination room – When you have found the proper room, you will be directed to the seat or part of the room where you will sit. Sometimes you are given a sheet of instructions to read while you are waiting. Do not fill out any forms until you are told to do so; just read them and be prepared.
- Relax and prepare to listen to the instructions
- If you have any physical problem that may keep you from doing your best, be sure to tell the test administrator. If you are sick or in poor health, you really cannot do your best on the exam. You can come back and take the test some other time.

VII. AT THE TEST

The day of the test is here and you have the test booklet in your hand. The temptation to get going is very strong. Caution! There is more to success than knowing the right answers. You must know how to identify your papers and understand variations in the type of short-answer question used in this particular examination. Follow these suggestions for maximum results from your efforts:

1) Cooperate with the monitor

The test administrator has a duty to create a situation in which you can be as much at ease as possible. He will give instructions, tell you when to begin, check to see that you are marking your answer sheet correctly, and so on. He is not there to guard you, although he will see that your competitors do not take unfair advantage. He wants to help you do your best.

2) Listen to all instructions

Don't jump the gun! Wait until you understand all directions. In most civil service tests you get more time than you need to answer the questions. So don't be in a hurry. Read each word of instructions until you clearly understand the meaning. Study the examples, listen to all announcements and follow directions. Ask questions if you do not understand what to do.

3) Identify your papers

Civil service exams are usually identified by number only. You will be assigned a number; you must not put your name on your test papers. Be sure to copy your number correctly. Since more than one exam may be given, copy your exact examination title.

4) Plan your time

Unless you are told that a test is a "speed" or "rate of work" test, speed itself is usually not important. Time enough to answer all the questions will be provided, but this does not mean that you have all day. An overall time limit has been set. Divide the total time (in minutes) by the number of questions to determine the approximate time you have for each question.

5) Do not linger over difficult questions

If you come across a difficult question, mark it with a paper clip (useful to have along) and come back to it when you have been through the booklet. One caution if you do this – be sure to skip a number on your answer sheet as well. Check often to be sure that you have not lost your place and that you are marking in the row numbered the same as the question you are answering.

6) Read the questions

Be sure you know what the question asks! Many capable people are unsuccessful because they failed to *read* the questions correctly.

7) Answer all questions

Unless you have been instructed that a penalty will be deducted for incorrect answers, it is better to guess than to omit a question.

8) Speed tests

It is often better NOT to guess on speed tests. It has been found that on timed tests people are tempted to spend the last few seconds before time is called in marking answers at random – without even reading them – in the hope of picking up a few extra points. To discourage this practice, the instructions may warn you that your score will be "corrected" for guessing. That is, a penalty will be applied. The incorrect answers will be deducted from the correct ones, or some other penalty formula will be used.

9) Review your answers

If you finish before time is called, go back to the questions you guessed or omitted to give them further thought. Review other answers if you have time.

10) Return your test materials

If you are ready to leave before others have finished or time is called, take ALL your materials to the monitor and leave quietly. Never take any test material with you. The monitor can discover whose papers are not complete, and taking a test booklet may be grounds for disqualification.

VIII. EXAMINATION TECHNIQUES

1) Read the general instructions carefully. These are usually printed on the first page of the exam booklet. As a rule, these instructions refer to the timing of the examination; the fact that you should not start work until the signal and must stop work at a signal, etc. If there are any *special* instructions, such as a choice of questions to be answered, make sure that you note this instruction carefully.

2) When you are ready to start work on the examination, that is as soon as the signal has been given, read the instructions to each question booklet, underline any key words or phrases, such as *least, best, outline, describe* and the like. In this way you will tend to answer as requested rather than discover on reviewing your paper that you *listed without describing*, that you selected the *worst* choice rather than the *best* choice, etc.

3) If the examination is of the objective or multiple-choice type – that is, each question will also give a series of possible answers: A, B, C or D, and you are called upon to select the best answer and write the letter next to that answer on your answer paper – it is advisable to start answering each question in turn. There may be anywhere from 50 to 100 such questions in the three or four hours allotted and you can see how much time would be taken if you read through all the questions before beginning to answer any. Furthermore, if you come across a question or group of questions which you know would be difficult to answer, it would undoubtedly affect your handling of all the other questions.

4) If the examination is of the essay type and contains but a few questions, it is a moot point as to whether you should read all the questions before starting to answer any one. Of course, if you are given a choice – say five out of seven and the like – then it is essential to read all the questions so you can eliminate the two that are most difficult. If, however, you are asked to answer all the questions, there may be danger in trying to answer the easiest one first because you may find that you will spend too much time on it. The best technique is to answer the first question, then proceed to the second, etc.

5) Time your answers. Before the exam begins, write down the time it started, then add the time allowed for the examination and write down the time it must be completed, then divide the time available somewhat as follows:
   - If 3-1/2 hours are allowed, that would be 210 minutes. If you have 80 objective-type questions, that would be an average of 2-1/2 minutes per question. Allow yourself no more than 2 minutes per question, or a total of 160 minutes, which will permit about 50 minutes to review.
   - If for the time allotment of 210 minutes there are 7 essay questions to answer, that would average about 30 minutes a question. Give yourself only 25 minutes per question so that you have about 35 minutes to review.

6) The most important instruction is to *read each question* and make sure you know what is wanted. The second most important instruction is to *time yourself properly* so that you answer every question. The third most important instruction is to *answer every question.* Guess if you have to but include something for each question. Remember that you will receive no credit for a blank and will probably receive some credit if you write something in answer to an essay question. If you guess a letter – say "B" for a multiple-choice question – you may have guessed right. If you leave a blank as an answer to a multiple-choice question, the examiners may respect your feelings but it will not add a point to your score. Some exams may penalize you for wrong answers, so in such cases *only*, you may not want to guess unless you have some basis for your answer.

7) Suggestions
   a. Objective-type questions
      1. Examine the question booklet for proper sequence of pages and questions
      2. Read all instructions carefully
      3. Skip any question which seems too difficult; return to it after all other questions have been answered
      4. Apportion your time properly; do not spend too much time on any single question or group of questions

5. Note and underline key words – *all, most, fewest, least, best, worst, same, opposite*, etc.
6. Pay particular attention to negatives
7. Note unusual option, e.g., unduly long, short, complex, different or similar in content to the body of the question
8. Observe the use of "hedging" words – *probably, may, most likely*, etc.
9. Make sure that your answer is put next to the same number as the question
10. Do not second-guess unless you have good reason to believe the second answer is definitely more correct
11. Cross out original answer if you decide another answer is more accurate; do not erase until you are ready to hand your paper in
12. Answer all questions; guess unless instructed otherwise
13. Leave time for review

b. Essay questions
1. Read each question carefully
2. Determine exactly what is wanted. Underline key words or phrases.
3. Decide on outline or paragraph answer
4. Include many different points and elements unless asked to develop any one or two points or elements
5. Show impartiality by giving pros and cons unless directed to select one side only
6. Make and write down any assumptions you find necessary to answer the questions
7. Watch your English, grammar, punctuation and choice of words
8. Time your answers; don't crowd material

8) Answering the essay question

Most essay questions can be answered by framing the specific response around several key words or ideas. Here are a few such key words or ideas:

M's: manpower, materials, methods, money, management
P's: purpose, program, policy, plan, procedure, practice, problems, pitfalls, personnel, public relations

a. Six basic steps in handling problems:
1. Preliminary plan and background development
2. Collect information, data and facts
3. Analyze and interpret information, data and facts
4. Analyze and develop solutions as well as make recommendations
5. Prepare report and sell recommendations
6. Install recommendations and follow up effectiveness

b. Pitfalls to avoid
1. *Taking things for granted* – A statement of the situation does not necessarily imply that each of the elements is necessarily true; for example, a complaint may be invalid and biased so that all that can be taken for granted is that a complaint has been registered

2. *Considering only one side of a situation* – Wherever possible, indicate several alternatives and then point out the reasons you selected the best one
3. *Failing to indicate follow up* – Whenever your answer indicates action on your part, make certain that you will take proper follow-up action to see how successful your recommendations, procedures or actions turn out to be
4. *Taking too long in answering any single question* – Remember to time your answers properly

IX. AFTER THE TEST

Scoring procedures differ in detail among civil service jurisdictions although the general principles are the same. Whether the papers are hand-scored or graded by machine we have described, they are nearly always graded by number. That is, the person who marks the paper knows only the number – never the name – of the applicant. Not until all the papers have been graded will they be matched with names. If other tests, such as training and experience or oral interview ratings have been given, scores will be combined. Different parts of the examination usually have different weights. For example, the written test might count 60 percent of the final grade, and a rating of training and experience 40 percent. In many jurisdictions, veterans will have a certain number of points added to their grades.

After the final grade has been determined, the names are placed in grade order and an eligible list is established. There are various methods for resolving ties between those who get the same final grade – probably the most common is to place first the name of the person whose application was received first. Job offers are made from the eligible list in the order the names appear on it. You will be notified of your grade and your rank as soon as all these computations have been made. This will be done as rapidly as possible.

People who are found to meet the requirements in the announcement are called "eligibles." Their names are put on a list of eligible candidates. An eligible's chances of getting a job depend on how high he stands on this list and how fast agencies are filling jobs from the list.

When a job is to be filled from a list of eligibles, the agency asks for the names of people on the list of eligibles for that job. When the civil service commission receives this request, it sends to the agency the names of the three people highest on this list. Or, if the job to be filled has specialized requirements, the office sends the agency the names of the top three persons who meet these requirements from the general list.

The appointing officer makes a choice from among the three people whose names were sent to him. If the selected person accepts the appointment, the names of the others are put back on the list to be considered for future openings.

That is the rule in hiring from all kinds of eligible lists, whether they are for typist, carpenter, chemist, or something else. For every vacancy, the appointing officer has his choice of any one of the top three eligibles on the list. This explains why the person whose name is on top of the list sometimes does not get an appointment when some of the persons lower on the list do. If the appointing officer chooses the second or third eligible, the No. 1 eligible does not get a job at once, but stays on the list until he is appointed or the list is terminated.

X. HOW TO PASS THE INTERVIEW TEST

The examination for which you applied requires an oral interview test. You have already taken the written test and you are now being called for the interview test – the final part of the formal examination.

You may think that it is not possible to prepare for an interview test and that there are no procedures to follow during an interview. Our purpose is to point out some things you can do in advance that will help you and some good rules to follow and pitfalls to avoid while you are being interviewed.

What is an interview supposed to test?

The written examination is designed to test the technical knowledge and competence of the candidate; the oral is designed to evaluate intangible qualities, not readily measured otherwise, and to establish a list showing the relative fitness of each candidate – as measured against his competitors – for the position sought. Scoring is not on the basis of "right" and "wrong," but on a sliding scale of values ranging from "not passable" to "outstanding." As a matter of fact, it is possible to achieve a relatively low score without a single "incorrect" answer because of evident weakness in the qualities being measured.

Occasionally, an examination may consist entirely of an oral test – either an individual or a group oral. In such cases, information is sought concerning the technical knowledges and abilities of the candidate, since there has been no written examination for this purpose. More commonly, however, an oral test is used to supplement a written examination.

Who conducts interviews?

The composition of oral boards varies among different jurisdictions. In nearly all, a representative of the personnel department serves as chairman. One of the members of the board may be a representative of the department in which the candidate would work. In some cases, "outside experts" are used, and, frequently, a businessman or some other representative of the general public is asked to serve. Labor and management or other special groups may be represented. The aim is to secure the services of experts in the appropriate field.

However the board is composed, it is a good idea (and not at all improper or unethical) to ascertain in advance of the interview who the members are and what groups they represent. When you are introduced to them, you will have some idea of their backgrounds and interests, and at least you will not stutter and stammer over their names.

What should be done before the interview?

While knowledge about the board members is useful and takes some of the surprise element out of the interview, there is other preparation which is more substantive. It *is* possible to prepare for an oral interview – in several ways:

1) Keep a copy of your application and review it carefully before the interview

This may be the only document before the oral board, and the starting point of the interview. Know what education and experience you have listed there, and the sequence and dates of all of it. Sometimes the board will ask you to review the highlights of your experience for them; you should not have to hem and haw doing it.

2) Study the class specification and the examination announcement

Usually, the oral board has one or both of these to guide them. The qualities, characteristics or knowledges required by the position sought are stated in these documents. They offer valuable clues as to the nature of the oral interview. For example, if the job involves supervisory responsibilities, the announcement will usually indicate that knowledge of modern supervisory methods and the qualifications of the candidate as a supervisor will be tested. If so, you can expect such questions, frequently in the form of a hypothetical situation which you are expected to solve. NEVER go into an oral without knowledge of the duties and responsibilities of the job you seek.

3) Think through each qualification required

Try to visualize the kind of questions you would ask if you were a board member. How well could you answer them? Try especially to appraise your own knowledge and background in each area, *measured against the job sought*, and identify any areas in which you are weak. Be critical and realistic – do not flatter yourself.

4) Do some general reading in areas in which you feel you may be weak

For example, if the job involves supervision and your past experience has NOT, some general reading in supervisory methods and practices, particularly in the field of human relations, might be useful. Do NOT study agency procedures or detailed manuals. The oral board will be testing your understanding and capacity, not your memory.

5) Get a good night's sleep and watch your general health and mental attitude

You will want a clear head at the interview. Take care of a cold or any other minor ailment, and of course, no hangovers.

What should be done on the day of the interview?

Now comes the day of the interview itself. Give yourself plenty of time to get there. Plan to arrive somewhat ahead of the scheduled time, particularly if your appointment is in the fore part of the day. If a previous candidate fails to appear, the board might be ready for you a bit early. By early afternoon an oral board is almost invariably behind schedule if there are many candidates, and you may have to wait. Take along a book or magazine to read, or your application to review, but leave any extraneous material in the waiting room when you go in for your interview. In any event, relax and compose yourself.

The matter of dress is important. The board is forming impressions about you – from your experience, your manners, your attitude, and your appearance. Give your personal appearance careful attention. Dress your best, but not your flashiest. Choose conservative, appropriate clothing, and be sure it is immaculate. This is a business interview, and your appearance should indicate that you regard it as such. Besides, being well groomed and properly dressed will help boost your confidence.

Sooner or later, someone will call your name and escort you into the interview room. *This is it.* From here on you are on your own. It is too late for any more preparation. But remember, you asked for this opportunity to prove your fitness, and you are here because your request was granted.

What happens when you go in?

The usual sequence of events will be as follows: The clerk (who is often the board stenographer) will introduce you to the chairman of the oral board, who will introduce you to the other members of the board. Acknowledge the introductions before you sit down. Do not be surprised if you find a microphone facing you or a stenotypist sitting by. Oral interviews are usually recorded in the event of an appeal or other review.

Usually the chairman of the board will open the interview by reviewing the highlights of your education and work experience from your application – primarily for the benefit of the other members of the board, as well as to get the material into the record. Do not interrupt or comment unless there is an error or significant misinterpretation; if that is the case, do not hesitate. But do not quibble about insignificant matters. Also, he will usually ask you some question about your education, experience or your present job – partly to get you to start talking and to establish the interviewing "rapport." He may start the actual questioning, or turn it over to one of the other members. Frequently, each member undertakes the questioning on a particular area, one in which he is perhaps most competent, so you can expect each member to participate in the examination. Because time is limited, you may also expect some rather abrupt switches in the direction the questioning takes, so do not be upset by it. Normally, a board member will not pursue a single line of questioning unless he discovers a particular strength or weakness.

After each member has participated, the chairman will usually ask whether any member has any further questions, then will ask you if you have anything you wish to add. Unless you are expecting this question, it may floor you. Worse, it may start you off on an extended, extemporaneous speech. The board is not usually seeking more information. The question is principally to offer you a last opportunity to present further qualifications or to indicate that you have nothing to add. So, if you feel that a significant qualification or characteristic has been overlooked, it is proper to point it out in a sentence or so. Do not compliment the board on the thoroughness of their examination – they have been sketchy, and you know it. If you wish, merely say, "No thank you, I have nothing further to add." This is a point where you can "talk yourself out" of a good impression or fail to present an important bit of information. Remember, *you close the interview yourself.*

The chairman will then say, "That is all, Mr. _______, thank you." Do not be startled; the interview is over, and quicker than you think. Thank him, gather your belongings and take your leave. Save your sigh of relief for the other side of the door.

How to put your best foot forward

Throughout this entire process, you may feel that the board individually and collectively is trying to pierce your defenses, seek out your hidden weaknesses and embarrass and confuse you. Actually, this is not true. They are obliged to make an appraisal of your qualifications for the job you are seeking, and they want to see you in your best light. Remember, they must interview all candidates and a non-cooperative candidate may become a failure in spite of their best efforts to bring out his qualifications. Here are 15 suggestions that will help you:

1) Be natural – Keep your attitude confident, not cocky

If you are not confident that you can do the job, do not expect the board to be. Do not apologize for your weaknesses, try to bring out your strong points. The board is interested in a positive, not negative, presentation. Cockiness will antagonize any board member and make him wonder if you are covering up a weakness by a false show of strength.

2) Get comfortable, but don't lounge or sprawl

Sit erectly but not stiffly. A careless posture may lead the board to conclude that you are careless in other things, or at least that you are not impressed by the importance of the occasion. Either conclusion is natural, even if incorrect. Do not fuss with your clothing, a pencil or an ashtray. Your hands may occasionally be useful to emphasize a point; do not let them become a point of distraction.

3) Do not wisecrack or make small talk

This is a serious situation, and your attitude should show that you consider it as such. Further, the time of the board is limited – they do not want to waste it, and neither should you.

4) Do not exaggerate your experience or abilities

In the first place, from information in the application or other interviews and sources, the board may know more about you than you think. Secondly, you probably will not get away with it. An experienced board is rather adept at spotting such a situation, so do not take the chance.

5) If you know a board member, do not make a point of it, yet do not hide it

Certainly you are not fooling him, and probably not the other members of the board. Do not try to take advantage of your acquaintanceship – it will probably do you little good.

6) Do not dominate the interview

Let the board do that. They will give you the clues – do not assume that you have to do all the talking. Realize that the board has a number of questions to ask you, and do not try to take up all the interview time by showing off your extensive knowledge of the answer to the first one.

7) Be attentive

You only have 20 minutes or so, and you should keep your attention at its sharpest throughout. When a member is addressing a problem or question to you, give him your undivided attention. Address your reply principally to him, but do not exclude the other board members.

8) Do not interrupt

A board member may be stating a problem for you to analyze. He will ask you a question when the time comes. Let him state the problem, and wait for the question.

9) Make sure you understand the question

Do not try to answer until you are sure what the question is. If it is not clear, restate it in your own words or ask the board member to clarify it for you. However, do not haggle about minor elements.

10) Reply promptly but not hastily

A common entry on oral board rating sheets is "candidate responded readily," or "candidate hesitated in replies." Respond as promptly and quickly as you can, but do not jump to a hasty, ill-considered answer.

11) Do not be peremptory in your answers

A brief answer is proper – but do not fire your answer back. That is a losing game from your point of view. The board member can probably ask questions much faster than you can answer them.

12) Do not try to create the answer you think the board member wants

He is interested in what kind of mind you have and how it works – not in playing games. Furthermore, he can usually spot this practice and will actually grade you down on it.

13) Do not switch sides in your reply merely to agree with a board member

Frequently, a member will take a contrary position merely to draw you out and to see if you are willing and able to defend your point of view. Do not start a debate, yet do not surrender a good position. If a position is worth taking, it is worth defending.

14) Do not be afraid to admit an error in judgment if you are shown to be wrong

The board knows that you are forced to reply without any opportunity for careful consideration. Your answer may be demonstrably wrong. If so, admit it and get on with the interview.

15) Do not dwell at length on your present job

The opening question may relate to your present assignment. Answer the question but do not go into an extended discussion. You are being examined for a *new* job, not your present one. As a matter of fact, try to phrase ALL your answers in terms of the job for which you are being examined.

Basis of Rating

Probably you will forget most of these "do's" and "don'ts" when you walk into the oral interview room. Even remembering them all will not ensure you a passing grade. Perhaps you did not have the qualifications in the first place. But remembering them will help you to put your best foot forward, without treading on the toes of the board members.

Rumor and popular opinion to the contrary notwithstanding, an oral board wants you to make the best appearance possible. They know you are under pressure – but they also want to see how you respond to it as a guide to what your reaction would be under the pressures of the job you seek. They will be influenced by the degree of poise you display, the personal traits you show and the manner in which you respond.

ABOUT THIS BOOK

This book contains tests divided into Examination Sections. Go through each test, answering every question in the margin. We have also attached a sample answer sheet at the back of the book that can be removed and used. At the end of each test look at the answer key and check your answers. On the ones you got wrong, look at the right answer choice and learn. Do not fill in the answers first. Do not memorize the questions and answers, but understand the answer and principles involved. On your test, the questions will likely be different from the samples. Questions are changed and new ones added. If you understand these past questions you should have success with any changes that arise. Tests may consist of several types of questions. We have additional books on each subject should more study be advisable or necessary for you. Finally, the more you study, the better prepared you will be. This book is intended to be the last thing you study before you walk into the examination room. Prior study of relevant texts is also recommended. NLC publishes some of these in our Fundamental Series. Knowledge and good sense are important factors in passing your exam. Good luck also helps. So now study this Passbook, absorb the material contained within and take that knowledge into the examination. Then do your best to pass that exam.

EXAMINATION SECTION

EXAMINATION SECTION
TEST 1

DIRECTIONS: Each question or incomplete statement is followed by several suggested answers or completions. Select the one that BEST answers the question or completes the statement. *PRINT THE LETTER OF THE CORRECT ANSWER IN THE SPACE AT THE RIGHT.*

1. What is a mulch? 1.____
A
   A. fertilizer which is high in nitrogen
   B. material spread upon the surface of the soil to conserve moisture and inhibit weed growth
   C. chemical compound which is sprayed on the foliage of plants to prevent wilting
   D. mixture of coarse gravel, stones, and broken rock used for drainage in the bottom of flower pots and planting tubs

2. A GOOD permanent grass seed mixture for a dry, shady lawn area is 2.____
   A. 2 parts Merion Blue grass, 1 part Kentucky Blue grass
   B. 1 part Merion Blue grass, 2 parts Rhode Island or Colonial Bent grass
   C. 1 part chewing fescue, 1 part Illahee fescue, 1 part Pennlawn fescue
   D. 2 part Perennial Rye grass, 1 part Italian Rye grass

3. Which of the following is the BEST cutting height for the average lawn in the city area in hot weather? 3.____
   A. 1/4" B. 1/2" C. 1" D. 2"

4. Earthworms are MOST likely to 4.____
   A. make good soil from poor soil
   B. make good soil into even better soil
   C. ruin good soil
   D. indicate a lack of organic matter in the soil

5. Before turning over a power rotary lawnmower to clean the underside and cutting blade, you SHOULD 5.____
   A. adjust the carburetor idle setting to low speed
   B. allow the engine to cool for at least 10 minutes
   C. remove the high-tension wire from the spark plug
   D. adjust the carburetor setting to full choke

6. A 10-6-4 fertilizer contains 6.____
   A. 4% nitrogen B. 10% potassium
   C. 6% potassium D. 6% phosphorus

7. Which of the following is *generally* the BEST pH range for a lawn soil? 7.____
pH
   A. 2-3.5 B. 3-4.5 C. 6-6.5 D. 8-10.5

8. Peat moss is BEST used as a(n) 8.___

A. mulch
B. organic soil amendment
C. fertilizer
D. substitute for lime

9. What does pH indicate? 9.___
The ______ the soil.

A. amount of nitrogen in
B. amount of moisture in
C. acidity or alkalinity of
D. amount of organic matter in

10. In order to promote dense growth on all parts of a hedge, it is BEST to prune it so that the 10.___

A. top is wider than the bottom
B. bottom is wider than the top
C. top and bottom are of equal width
D. top and bottom are narrower than the middle

11. When should shrubs that bloom in the spring, such as Weigela and Lilac *generally* be pruned? 11.___

A. As soon as they are finished blooming
B. Just before they bloom
C. While they are blooming
D. When they are still dormant

12. Assume that you wish to cut a large limb off a tree trunk. In order to do this without damage to the tree, the MINIMUM number of separate saw cuts which should *usually* be made is 12.___

A. 1
B. 2
C. 3
D. 4

13. The BEST method of controlling infestations of scale insects on young trees is by 13.___

A. dusting the trees with a good fungicide
B. removing and burning affected limbs and branches
C. digging up and destroying the trees
D. spraying the trees with dormant oil

14. In a slat house for shading plants, the direction in which the roof slats should run is a(n) ______ direction. 14.___

A. east-west
B. north-south
C. northeast by southwest
D. northwest by southeast

15. Which one of the following plants is a monocotyledon? 15.___

A. Begonia
B. Geranium
C. Phlox
D. Iris

16. You are in charge of a small lawn area of 1850 sq.ft. You are asked to apply lime on this lawn at the rate of 40 pounds per 1000 sq.ft. 16.____
The number of pounds of lime you will need to cover the entire area of the lawn is MOST NEARLY ______ lbs.

A. 85 B. 86 C. 87 D. 89

17. A Kentucky Blue grass lawn requires 3 lbs. of actual nitrogen per 1000 square feet. How many pounds of 10-6-4 fertilizer will be needed to fertilize a 5000 square foot lawn of Kentucky Blue grass? ______ lbs. 17.____

A. 15.5 B. 150 C. 555 D. 50

18. You need to fill a 32-oz. bottle with a solution contain-10% malathion, but all you have is a gallon of 50% malathion solution. 18.____
How many ounces of the 50% malathion solution and how many ounces of water should you put in the bottle? ______ oz. of 50% malathion solution and ______ oz. of water.

A. 3.2; 28.8 B. 6.4; 25.6
C. 9.6; 22.4 D. 12.8; 19.2

19. The term *hardiness* is MOST often used to refer to the 19.____
A. tensile strength of the plant's stem and branches
B. ability of plants to endure low temperatures
C. amount of wind force the plant can withstand
D. length of time that plant can survive without water

20. Which one of the following is NOT a method of plant propagation? 20.____

A. Layering B. Budding C. Chlorosis D. Division

KEY (CORRECT ANSWERS)

1.	B	11.	A
2.	C	12.	C
3.	D	13.	D
4.	B	14.	B
5.	C	15.	D
6.	D	16.	A
7.	C	17.	B
8.	B	18.	B
9.	C	19.	B
10.	B	20.	C

TEST 2

DIRECTIONS: Each question or incomplete statement is followed by several suggested answers or completions. Select the one that BEST answers the question or completes the statement. *PRINT THE LETTER OF THE CORRECT ANSWER IN THE SPACE AT THE RIGHT.*

1. Clematis, wisteria, and ampelopsis are ALL 1.____

   A. indoor foliage plants
   B. outdoor annuals
   C. grown from bulbs planted each fall
   D. ornamental climbing plants

2. In attaching a scion to a stock, you should use which one of the following methods? 2.____

   A. Whip or tongue
   B. Tack weld
   C. Pintle and gudgeon
   D. Clinch or rivet and burr

3. *Pinching*, as performed by a gardener, is a method of 3.____

   A. grafting
   B. pruning
   C. propagation
   D. pollination

4. In a project involving the laying of sod, the soil was properly cultivated, fertilized, and the turf laid and rolled in the approved fashion. Water was periodically applied in ample quantity. After a few days, the grass began to die around the edges of each rectangular piece of sod. 4.____
   The BEST method of avoiding such a problem is *probably* to

   A. add more fertilizer to the soil before the turf is laid
   B. apply lime before and after the sod has been laid
   C. brush a dressing of sandy loam into the joints between the sods
   D. water the sod only in bright sunlight

5. A label on a plant was marked as follows: Abie nobilis glauca, Pinaceae. 5.____
   The name of this plant reveals that the

   A. species is Abies, the genus is nobilis, the family is glauca, and the variety is Pinaceae
   B. family is Abies, the variety is nobilis, the genus is glauca, and the species is Pinaceae
   C. genus is Abies, the family is nobilis, the species is glauca, and the variety is Pinaceae
   D. genus is Abies, the species is Nobilis, the variety is glauca, and the family is Pinaceae

6. A small deciduous tree in leaf has just been dug from the ground and transplanted into a tub and then watered until the soil is saturated. It quickly shows symptoms of severe wilting. 6.____
   In trying to save this tree, which of the following would be the LEAST acceptable remedy?

A. Remove some of the foliage, either by removing some of the leaves or some of the smaller branches with their foliage
B. Wet the plant's foliage and then place a plastic bag over the entire tree and place it either in a shady place or a darkened room
C. Remove the tree from the tub and remove all of the soil from the roots and then place the plant in a pail of water so the roots are completely submerged
D. Place the tree under the constant mist of a fine water spray

7. A certain broad-leaf evergreen tree had many flowers in the spring but it bore no fruit in the fall. The next spring a close examination of the flowers revealed only stamens and no pistils. 7.____
The *probable* reason for the failure of the tree to fruit is that the

A. flowers were deformed
B. tree was a male
C. tree was a female and there was no male in the vicinity
D. tree was planted too far north and the cold weather prevented it from fruiting

8. Which one of the following trees would be LEAST desirable for planting in a shady area? 8.____

A. Dogwood B. Pine C. Hemlock D. Holly

9. Brown patches are noticed in a sunny lawn area in the summer. A close examination reveals numerous brown insects around the grass roots in the patches about 1/6" long with white markings on their backs. 9.____
These insects MOST likely are

A. aphids
B. scale insects
C. chinch bugs
D. leaf hoppers

10. Many diseases of lawn grasses can be treated effectively with 10.____

A. Benomyl (Benlate)
B. 2,4-D
C. DDT
D. Rotenone

11. Of the following, the BEST way to reduce the acidity of soil is to apply 11.____

A. limestone
B. flowers of sulfur
C. aluminum sulfate
D. water

12. The MOST effective of the following actions to take to stop erosion of soil on steep embankments is to 12.____

A. break the flow of water on the embankment
B. dig several water channels from the top of the embankment to the bottom
C. rototill the embankment
D. spray the embankment with 2,4-D

13. A *complete* fertilizer contains 13.____

A. nitrogen, phosphorus, and iron
B. calcium, potassium, and sulfur
C. nitrogen, phosphorus, and potassium
D. calcium, carbon, and nitrogen

14. Plants produce seeds by means of 14.____

A. pollination and fertilization
B. cultivation and grafting
C. hybridization and air-layering
D. rooting and hydrogenation

15. If a tree is to be replanted in a heavy clay-loam soil with questionable drainage, it would be BEST to plant the tree 15.____

A. three inches deeper than it was planted before
B. six inches deeper than it was planted before
C. at the same level as before and backfill with sand
D. slightly higher in the soil than it was planted before

16. Suckers are MOST likely to develop from 16.____

A. buds
B. roots
C. shoots
D. leaf cuttings

17. All of the following are piercing-sucking insects EXCEPT the 17.____

A. white fly
B. leaf hopper
C. lace bug
D. black vine weevil

18. Knowing and using good horticultural books for reference is important in gardening work. Which of the following is a GOOD horticultural book? 18.____

A. HORTUS SECOND, by Liberty Hyde Bailey
B. PLANT LOCATION IN THEORY AND IN PRACTICE, by Melvin Greenhut
C. HOW GREEN WAS MY VALLEY, by Richard Llewellyn
D. THE GREENING OF AMERICA, by Charles Reich

19. The pine bark aphid is a pest of pines such as the Eastern White Pine (Pinus strobus). A superior-type emulsifiable oil spray can be applied during the early spring when the tree is still dormant. 19.____
Which of the following conditions are BEST for applying the spray?

A. There is no wind, the day temperature is 50° F or higher, the night temperature is above the mid 30's, no rain is predicted
B. A slight wind is predicted, the day temperature does not exceed 48° F, the night temperature is predicted to fall below freezing
C. A slight wind is predicted, the day temperature and the night temperature are both above 85° F, and the day is misty
D. The aphids start to move

20. An excellent fungicide which not only has historical significance but is still highly recommended for control of certain fungus diseases contains copper sulfate, hydrated lime, and water. 20.____
This fungicide is called

A. Ferbam
B. Bordeaux mixture
C. Solution C.S.H.L.
D. Captan

KEY (CORRECT ANSWERS)

1. D
2. A
3. B
4. C
5. D
6. C
7. B
8. B
9. C
10. A
11. A
12. A
13. C
14. A
15. D
16. A
17. D
18. A
19. A
20. B

TEST 3

DIRECTIONS: Each question or incomplete statement is followed by several suggested answers or completions. Select the one that BEST answers the question or completes the statement. *PRINT THE LETTER OF THE CORRECT ANSWER IN THE SPACE AT THE RIGHT.*

1. A heavy mulch is LEAST desirable for 1.____

   A. iris
   B. rhododendrons
   C. azaleas
   D. newly planted trees

2. You have noticed that a number of older leaves fall each year from a pine tree. This phenomenon is *probably* due to 2.____

   A. root rot
   B. insufficient fertilizer
   C. natural aging of the needles
   D. insufficient water

3. The BEST time to sow grass seed in the city is 3.____

   A. mid-August to mid-September
   B. mid-March to mid-April
   C. late April to mid-May
   D. late May to early June

4. In order to maintain natural growth, the BEST of the following methods of pruning forsythia is to remove 4.____

   A. half of the top growth
   B. only the apical buds
   C. up to one-third of the older stems
   D. all growth over two feet

5. Which one of the following trees can be *safely* pruned in spring when sap is flowing? 5.____

   A. Acer saccharium - Sugar Maple
   B. Ulmus species - Elms
   C. Cladrastis lutea - Yellow-wood
   D. Pinus thumbergii - Japanese Black Pine

6. Of the following, the BEST way to treat trees or shrubs with dead and diseased branches is to 6.____

   A. leave them alone
   B. prune to remove 1/3 of older wood
   C. prune back to healthy wood
   D. spray with 2,4-D

7. Anthracnose disease of Plantanus species (Plane trees) is more prevalent in wet spring weather.
   This disease is caused by a 7.____

   A. beetle
   B. fungus
   C. mildew
   D. gas leak

8. Peat moss is frequently used in gardening to change soil conditions. Which of the following is the BEST definition of peat moss? 8.____

   A. A short, slow-growing plant
   B. Completely decomposed animal life
   C. Partially decomposed plant life
   D. A type of wood

9. A sprayer which has been used to spray insecticides and will be used for this purpose in the future should NEVER be used to apply 9.____

   A. fungicides
   B. miticides
   C. malathion
   D. herbicides

10. It is especially important that an excess of fertilizer not be applied to the soil because of the possibility of root damage. This is due to the fact that fertilizer is a(n) 10.____

   A. acid
   B. base
   C. salt
   D. alkali

11. Of the following, the BEST time to apply fertilizer to lawn grasses is *usually* when the 11.____

   A. soil is *moist* and the grass is *wet*
   B. grass is *dry* and the soil is *moist*
   C. soil and the grass are *dry*
   D. soil is *dry* and the grass is *wet*

12. Assume that a child's rope swing has been attached to a tree by tying the rope securely around the lowest limb. Of the following, it is MOST important that 12.____

   A. girdling of the limb at the point of attachment of the rope does not eventually occur
   B. only a natural fiber rope is used
   C. the rope be lengthened as the tree grows in height
   D. as the limb grows in length, the swing be moved back toward the trunk to adjust for linear growth

13. An established lawn which requires watering during dry periods should be watered 13.____

   A. *lightly* twice a day in the morning and again at dusk
   B. *lightly* once a day in the morning unless the humidity is above 90%
   C. *thoroughly* to a depth of at least 4 inches early in the day
   D. *thoroughly* to a depth of 4 inches in the morning and again at dusk

14. A Rhododendron shows severe yellowing of leaves. The problem is due to an iron deficiency. To correct this deficiency, it is MOST effective to apply iron 14.____

   A. carbide
   B. pyrites
   C. chelate
   D. oxide

15. The color of the flower of some species of plants is distinctly affected by soil alkalinity or acidity as well as the amount of aluminum or iron in the soil. When the soil is neutral or alkaline, the flower color is pinker, whereas under acid soil conditions the flower color is bluer. Which one of the following plants is BEST known to exhibit this response? 15.____

A. Rose species - Roses
B. Hydrangea macrophylla (hortensis) - House Hydrangea
C. Chrysanthemum morifolium - Florist and Garden Chrysanthemums
D. Begonia semperflorens - wax or fibrous-rooted begonias

16. Which one of the following terms refers to a method in which trees or shrubs can be trained into a special shape or form? 16.____

A. Abscission
B. Layering
C. Pricking-out
D. Espalier

17. Which one of the following is NOT a shrub? 17.____

A. Pieris japonica
B. Abelia grandiflora
C. Acer platanoides
D. Viburnum japonicum

18. You have just been told by your supervisor that your crew members must use a new method for accounting for the time spent on specific jobs. Some members of your crew complain to you that the previous method was better. 18.____
Of the following, the BEST action to take FIRST is to

A. find out specifically to what your crew objects
B. suggest to your crew members that they are correct and that management does not really understand the effect of the change
C. tell your crew to try the new method and that if they still feel that way in a few weeks they can go back to the old method
D. take a vote among your crew to determine which method to use

19. Complaining to your crew about working conditions is 19.____

A. *advisable* ; it makes you
B. *advisable;* it allows you to get your feelings out in the open
C. *inadvisable,* it permits the crew to depend more on the attitudes and approval of their supervisor
D. *inadvisable,* it brings attention to problems but does not resolve them

20. Asking your crew for their suggestions on better gardening methods is 20.____

A. *inadvisable;* they may feel that you lack self-confidence
B. *inadvisable;* it is poor practice to become too friendly with those you supervise
C. *advisable;* it makes the men feel they have a hand in decision making
D. *advisable;* those who make the suggestions can be held responsible for results

KEY (CORRECT ANSWERS)

1.	A	11.	B
2.	C	12.	A
3.	A	13.	C
4.	C	14.	C
5.	D	15.	B
6.	C	16.	D
7.	B	17.	C
8.	C	18.	A
9.	D	19.	D
10.	C	20.	C

TEST 4

DIRECTIONS: Each question or incomplete statement is followed by several suggested answers or completions. Select the one that BEST answers the question or completes the statement. *PRINT THE LETTER OF THE CORRECT ANSWER IN THE SPACE AT THE RIGHT.*

1. For you, as a supervisor, to explain department objectives for the year ahead to a new employee is 1.____

   A. *inadvisable;* the new employee may leave before the year is up
   B. *inadvisable;* the new employee has nothing to do with the goals of the department
   C. *advisable;* it may enable the new employee to do the job with less training
   D. *advisable;* it may give the new employee a sense of personal involvement and motivation

2. When a new laborer reports for duty for the first time, which of the following should be discussed with him FIRST? 2.____

   A. Departmental rules and regulations that relate to his employment
   B. The priorities that he should assign to his work
   C. The latest techniques of getting the technical work done
   D. The recognition of what constitutes an error in his work and its consequences

3. While you are trimming some shrubs in the park, a woman comes up to you and tells you that her civic club is running a benefit for the handicapped and that it would be wonderful if the department would donate some flowers to this worthy cause. You do not know how this type of situation has been handled in the past. 3.____
   Of the following, the BEST action for you to take is to tell the woman that you

   A. are sure the department will be happy to donate flowers, and take her name and address
   B. have nothing to do with department policy and cannot make that decision
   C. are not sure what the department policy is but you think she is wasting her time trying to get flowers from the department
   D. are not sure what department policy is but that you will tell her how to get more information

4. One of your crew members has made an error in the care of bulbs, resulting in the loss of many expensive bulbs. 4.____
   Of the following, the BEST way to handle this situation *initially* is to

   A. write a memo on the care of bulbs and post it where your crew can refer to it
   B. call your crew together and discuss the proper care of bulbs
   C. speak privately to the crew member who made the error and discuss his error and proper care of bulbs with him
   D. tell the crew member who made the error you will not report him at present, but if this type of error occurs again you will recommend his dismissal

5. It has been brought to your attention that several expensive tools are missing from the tool cabinet. Since this had never before been a problem, the cabinet was always left unlocked. 5.____
   Of the following, the BEST way to handle this situation is to

A. lock the cabinet, and give keys to all your crew members, making them all responsible for the tools
B. lock the cabinet, and make one of your crew members responsible for the key to the cabinet and the tools inside
C. announce to your crew members that if a tool is missing they will all have to be charged an appropriate amount towards the purchase of a new tool
D. assign each crew member a particular tool and have him use this device exclusively

6. Of the following, the BEST reason for the practice of requiring your crew members to sign in and out for lunch is that 6.____

A. the crew members are more productive when they are more strictly controlled
B. it enables the supervisor to regulate the time and working hours of the crew members more directly
C. it will prevent crew members from leaving the work area during their lunch period
D. the supervisor will find out the preferred lunch period for each individual crew member

7. While pruning some shrubs, a crew member under your supervision trips over what he thinks was a loose cobblestone. After checking to make sure he has suffered no injury, of the following, the MOST advisable action for you to take NEXT is to 7.____

A. tell him to be more careful in the future
B. determine what actually caused the accident
C. post safety rules where they can be seen by all crew members
D. assign him to a different type of work at another location

8. One of the crew members under your supervision tells you that the lawnmower he has been using has just broken down. Of the following, the BEST reason for you to try operating the mower yourself is to 8.____

A. test the worker's knowledge with his performance on the job
B. keep the machines in need of repair in service as long as possible
C. show that supervisors can do the work of the crew members
D. determine whether a minor adjustment will bring the machine to operating condition

9. You have just explained to your most competent crew member a complicated root-pruning procedure that you wish him to follow. He tells you that he is a little uncertain about it and is not sure he can handle it.
Of the following, the BEST action for you to take is to 9.____

A. show him how much confidence you have in him by leaving him alone to do the job
B. have another crew member work with him to make sure that the job is done correctly
C. stay with him while he does the job to assure yourself that he knows how to do it correctly
D. drop the assignment until such time as he indicates that he is ready for it

10. While you are replanting some flowers, a man comes up to you and starts berating you for the condition of the park.
Of the following, the BEST way to handle this situation is to 10.____

A. suggest that he write to the department about his complaint
B. ask the man to leave and call for a police officer if he does not
C. explain to the man that those who use the park are primarily responsible for its condition
D. tell him that his opinions about the conditions of the park are wrong

11. Gardeners should be courteous to the public PRIMARILY because 11.____

A. someone might report them if they are not
B. this might earn them a merit increase
C. a good relationship between the department and the public is important
D. this makes for better morale among their crew members

12. Assume that you have been asked to evaluate the performance of one of your crew members. 12.____
The one of the following which should be given the LEAST consideration when making this evaluation is the employee's attitude towards

A. his co-workers
B. the organization
C. his friends
D. you

Questions 13-15.

DIRECTIONS: Questions 13 through 15 are to be answered on the basis of the following report.

To: *John Greene*
General Park Foreman

Date: May 5

From: *Earl Jones*
Gardener

Subject:

On May 3rd, as I was finishing a job six feet from the boathouse, I observed that the hole which had been filled in last week was now not level with the ground around it. This seems to be a hazardous condition because it might cause pedestrians to fall into it. I, therefore, suggest that this job be redone as soon as possible.

13. This report should be considered *poorly* written MAINLY because 13.____

A. it does not give enough information to take appropriate action
B. too many different tenses are used
C. it describes no actual personal injury to anyone
D. there is no recommendation in the report to remedy the situation

14. It is noted that the subject of the report has been left out. 14.____
Which of the following statements would be BEST as the subject of this report?

A. Observation made by Earl Jones, Gardener
B. Deteriorating condition of park grounds
C. Report of dangerous condition near boathouse
D. A dangerous walk through the park

15. In order for John Greene to take *appropriate action,* ADDITIONAL information should be added to the report giving the 15.____

    A. exact date the repair was made
    B. exact location of the hole
    C. exact time the observation was made
    D. names of the crew who previously filled in the hole

Questions 16-20.

DIRECTIONS: Questions 16 through 20 are based on the Fact Situation and the Repair Request Report form below. Read the Fact Situation carefully and examine the blank report form. Questions 16 through 20 ask how the report form should be filled in based on the information given in the Fact Situation.

FACT SITUATION

John Smith is a gardener, permanently assigned to the greenhouse in Queens. On Tuesday morning, he arrives at the greenhouse at 8 A.M. and sees that seven panes of glass in the west wing of the greenhouse have been broken. Since several large rooks are found on the greenhouse floor, it appears that the panes of the windows have been broken by vandals. It is necessary to repair the windows immediately due to the cold weather. In order to arrange for the repair, John Smith must complete the following "Repair Request Report."

REPAIR REQUEST REPORT

1. *Date of Request* ____________ 2. *Time* ________
3. *Location of Needed Repair* ____________
4. *Type of Repair Requested* ____________
5. *Reason for Request* ____________

____

6. *Signed* ____________ 7. *Title* ____________
8. *Additional Comments* ____________

____

16. Which of the following should be entered in Blank 4? 16.____

    A. Rock removal
    B. Broken glass
    C. Window pane replacement
    D. Heater installation

17. Based on the information given in the Pact Situation, it is *impossible* to fill in which one of the following blanks? 17.____
    Blank ______.

    A. 1
    B. 3
    C. 5
    D. 7

18. Which of the following would it be MOST appropriate to include in Blank 8? 18.____

A. John Smith was on time for work on January 10, 1997.
B. It seems that the windows were broken by vandals.
C. The weather forecast for the next few days is unknown.
D. Identity of vandals is unknown.

19. Of the following, the BEST way for John Smith to show his supervisor that the Repair Request Report was properly filled out is to 19.____

A. personally deliver the report to the repair crew
B. have two signatures instead of one required in Blank 6
C. show his supervisor a duplicate copy of the report
D. in Blank 8 include the dimensions of the panes of glass needed

20. It is necessary to emphasize the need to have the repair made quickly. The PROPER blank on the form to show the urgency of this request is Blank 20.____

A. 2 B. 3 C. 7 D. '8

KEY (CORRECT ANSWERS)

1.	D	11.	C
2.	A	12.	C
3.	D	13.	A
4.	C	14.	C
5.	B	15.	B
6.	B	16.	C
7.	B	17.	A
8.	D	18.	B
9.	C	19.	C
10.	A	20.	D

EXAMINATION SECTION
TEST 1

DIRECTIONS: Each question or incomplete statement is followed by several suggested answers or completions. Select the one that BEST answers the question or completes the statement. *PRINT THE LETTER OF THE CORRECT ANSWER IN THE SPACE AT THE RIGHT.*

1. A disadvantage of DDT was that it 1.____

   A. was not effective against sucking insects
   B. was not effective against chewing insects
   C. destroyed the roots of most flowering plants
   D. destroyed the natural enemies of various mites

2. A characteristic of chlordane is that it 2.____

   A. does not act as a contact poison
   B. does not act as a stomach poison
   C. has long-lasting effects
   D. is slow-acting

3. For a soil test, it is BEST to dig the samples of soil in the 3.____

   A. early spring
   B. summer
   C. early fall
   D. winter

4. The symbol used to indicate soil acidity is 4.____

   A. AC
   B. Hp
   C. pH
   D. SA

5. Loam is a type of soil that 5.____

   A. contains no organic matter
   B. is coarser than clay
   C. is coarser than sand
   D. is usually unfertile

6. Urea is a form of 6.____

   A. iron
   B. nitrogen
   C. phosphorus
   D. potassium

7. The one of the following which is NOT a source of potash is 7.____

   A. steamed bone meal
   B. wood ashes
   C. potassium chloride
   D. potassium sulphate

8. A good organic source of nitrogen is 8.____

   A. ammonium sulphate
   B. nitrate of soda
   C. bone meal
   D. dried blood

9. Which one of these statements about a 4-12-4 fertilizer is TRUE? 9.____
   The ______ number shows the percentage of ______.

   A. first; phosphorus
   B. first; potassium
   C. last; potash
   D. second; nitrogen

10. Which one of the following is NOT alkaline in its reaction? 10.____

A. Ammonium phosphate
B. Calcium nitrate
C. Cyanamide
D. Wood ashes

11. The addition of which one of the following will be LEAST likely to make the soil more acid? 11.____

A. Aluminum sulphate
B. Lime
C. Oak leafmold
D. Sawdust

12. What is the action of superphosphate applied to the soil as a top dressing? 12.____
It

A. does not penetrate the soil
B. penetrates the soil very slowly
C. penetrates the soil moderately fast
D. penetrates the soil very quickly

13. A disadvantage in using raw bone meal as a fertilizer is that it(its) 13.____

A. increases the soil acidity over a period of years
B. is unsafe for use on most plants
C. nitrogen content is very slowly available to plants
D. phosphorus content is very slowly available to plants

14. An advantage of a commercial fertilizer over an animal manure is that a commercial fertilizer 14.____

A. has a higher percentage of plant nutrients
B. adds to the organic content of the soil
C. greatly increases bacterial activity in the soil
D. will not burn plant roots

15. A characteristic of compost is that it 15.____

A. decreases slightly the amount of plant nutrient in the soil
B. decreases slightly the humus content of the soil
C. improves soil texture in flower gardens
D. is naturally free of weed seeds

16. As compared to a sandy soil, a characteristic of a clay soil is that it is 16.____

A. able to hold less water
B. harder to work when wet
C. quicker in drying out in the spring
D. quicker to warm up in the spring

17. A POOR way to improve the structure of a sandy soil is to add 17.____

A. compost
B. humus
C. organic matter
D. sand

18. For BEST growth, azaleas require a soil that is 18.____

A. neutral
B. either alkaline or neutral
C. alkaline
D. acid

19. Which one of the following is the LEAST acceptable procedure when transplanting trees? 19.____

    A. Prune the top back about one-fourth.
    B. Root prune a large tree for at least one growing season before it is transplanted.
    C. Transplant in the spring or the fall.
    D. Transplant only large trees because they can withstand the shock of transplanting better.

20. When a deciduous shrub is dug with a ball of earth for transplanting from one location to another, the size of the ball of earth should USUALLY be about ______ the spread of the branches. 20.____

    A. twice B. 1 1/2 times
    C. equal to D. one-half

21. Which of the following is true about California privet but NOT about Japanese Barberry? It 21.____

    A. is suitable for use as a hedge material
    B. requires little clipping for a neat appearance
    C. grows very tall
    D. is thorny

22. Outdoor fall planting is NOT recommended for 22.____

    A. dahlias B. hyacinths
    C. lilies-of-the-valley D. tulips

23. A characteristic of plants classified as annuals is that they usually 23.____

    A. grow well on any soil
    B. grow well only on considerably acid soil
    C. are shade-loving
    D. are sun-loving

24. The recommended spacing between sweet pea plants is ______ inches. 24.____

    A. over 24 B. 18 - 24 C. 6 - 12 D. 1 - 4

25. To say that a seed is *viable* means that it 25.____

    A. is subject to fungus disease
    B. is subject to insect damage
    C. can take root and grow
    D. cannot grow in moist soils

26. A characteristic of Merion Kentucky blue grass is that it 26.____

    A. is highly susceptible to leafspot
    B. needs heavy watering daily
    C. will thrive on close cutting
    D. germinates quickly

27. Fertilization of bluegrass and fescue grasses in the summer is 27.____

    A. *desirable* because the usual dryness of this season requires increased feeding to offset the shortage of moisture
    B. *not desirable* because there is more chance of burning the grass
    C. *desirable* because this is the period of their most active growth
    D. *not desirable* because they are semi-dormant and fertilization will stimulate weed growth

28. Serious and widespread diseases of lawn grasses are caused MOSTLY by 28.____

    A. algae B. bacteria C. crabgrass D. fungi

29. Anthracnose is a type of 29.____

    A. worm B. insect pest
    C. lawn grass D. fungus disease

Questions 30-33.

DIRECTIONS: Each of Questions 30 through 33 gives the name of a fumigant or an insecticide which may be classified under one of the headings in Column I. For each fumigant or insecticide, select the heading from Column I under which it is MOST correctly classified and print the letter in the space at the right.

COLUMN I

A. a plant insecticide non-poisonous to man
B. a plant insecticide poisonous to man
C. a soil fumigant which should not be used on plants

30. Arsenate of lead 30.____
31. Chloropicrin 31.____
32. Pyrethrum 32.____
33. Rotenone 33.____

Questions 34-37.

DIRECTIONS: Each of Questions 34 through 37 gives the name of an insect which may be classified under one of the headings in Column II. For each insect, select the heading from Column II under which it is MOST correctly classified and print the letter in the space at the right.

COLUMN II

A. insect beneficial to plants
B. insect injurious to plants
C. insect neither beneficial nor injurious to plants

34. Syrphid fly 34.____
35. Lady beetle (lady bug) 35.____
36. Grasshopper 36.____
37. Aphid 37.____

Questions 38-41.

DIRECTIONS: Each of Questions 38 through 41 gives the name of a weed. For each weed, select the BEST weed killer from Column III and print the letter in the space at the right.

	COLUMN III	
38. Speedwells (Veronica)	A. 2,4-D	38.____
39. Plantain	B. 2,4,5 - TP (Silvex)	39.____
40. Dandelion	C. Endothal	40.____
41. Chickweed		41.____

Questions 42-44.

DIRECTIONS: In areas where it is difficult to establish and maintain grass, such as on slopes and in deep shade, the planting of a ground cover plant is recommended. Questions 42 through 44 give the names of 3 ground cover plants. Select from Column IV the descriptive statement that is MOST applicable to each one and print the letter in the space at the right.

	COLUMN IV	
42. English ivy	A. small, dark green, glossy leaves; violet blue flowers B. trailing evergreen vine	42.____
43. Japanese pachysandra	C. spreads by suckers; greenish-white flowers; plants about 8 inches high	43.____
44. Myrtle	D. a bunch-growing member of the lily family; 8-12 inches high; purple to white flowers	44.____

Questions 45-48.

DIRECTIONS: Each of Questions 45 through 48 gives the name of a mulch which may be classified under one of the headings in Column V. For each mulch, select the heading from Column V under which it Is MOST correctly classified and print the letter in the space at the right.

	COLUMN V	
45. Peat moss	A. acid mulch	45.____
46. Grass clippings	B. non-acid mulch	46.____
47. Decayed pine needles		47.____
48. Corn cobs		48.____

Questions 49-53.

DIRECTIONS: Questions 49 through 53 give the names of 5 lawn grasses. For each grass, select the statement from Column VI that is MOST applicable and print the letter in the space at the right.

COLUMN VI

49. Meyer Zoysia
50. Bentgrass
51. Rough bluegrass
52. Red fescue
53. Kentucky bluegrass

A. used mainly for golf course putting greens
B. best grass for sunny places in good soil
C. suitable for moist, shady areas
D. turns brown in fall till mid-spring
E. best grass for dry soil, sun or shade

49.___ 50.___ 51.___ 52.___ 53.___

Questions 54-58.

DIRECTIONS: Questions 54 through 58 give the names of 5 shrubs. Classify each shrub according to height as in Column VII and print the letter in the space at the right.

COLUMN VII

54. Thunberg spirea
55. Japanese adromeda
56. Tartarian honeysuckle
57. Slender deutzia
58. Shrub Althea

A. low shrub - about 3 feet in height
B. medium shrub - about 5 feet in height
C. tall shrub - about 8 feet or more in height

54.___ 55.___ 56.___ 57.___ 58.___

Questions 59-62.

DIRECTIONS: Questions 59 through 62 give the names of 4 pairs of shrubs. Classify each pair of shrubs according to the scheme shown in Column VIII and print the letter in the space at the right.

COLUMN VIII

59. Sweet mockorange - snowhill hydrangea — A. both shrubs are deciduous — 59.____

60. Dwarf Japanese yew - pyramidal arborvitae — B. both shrubs are evergreen — 60.____

61. Mountain adromeda - Pfitzer juniper — C. one shrub is deciduous and one shrub is evergreen — 61.____

62. Mountain laurel - fragrant viburnum — 62.____

Questions 63-68.

DIRECTIONS: Questions 63 through 68 give the names of shrubs. Column IX gives suggested times for pruning shrubs. For each shrub in Questions 63 through 68, select from Column IX the BEST time to prune it and print the letter in the space at the right.

COLUMN IX

63. Vanhoutte's spirea — A. prune in spring after flowering — 63.____

64. Rose of sharon — B. prune in fall after flowering — 64.____

65. Peegee hydrangea — 65.____

66. Common lilac — 66.____

67. Buddleja — 67.____

68. Just before seeding a new lawn on average soil, a 5-10-5 fertilizer should be applied at the rate of ______ pounds for every 1,000 square feet. 68.____

A. 100 B. 75 C. 40 D. 20

69. Compared with the hydraulic sprayer, the mist blower 69.____

A. causes more loss of spray material from dripping
B. is always preferred in areas inaccessible to heavy equipment
C. is less affected by windy weather
D. requires greater skill by the operator

70. A gardener stands a 24-foot ladder against an upright tree trunk. To safely use the ladder, the distance between the base of the tree trunk and the foot of the ladder should be APPROXIMATELY ______feet(inches). 70.____

A. 8 B. 2 C. 3 D. 6

71. Reel power mowers, as contrasted with rotary power mowers, 71.____

A. are easier to control
B. cause fewer accidents
C. cost less
D. are closer to trees

72. To hold an electric hedge cutter with both hands when using it is considered 72.____

A. *good* procedure because it lessens the severity of electric shocks
B. *poor* procedure because it increases the likelihood of receiving electric shocks
C. *good* procedure because it reduces the chance of an accident
D. *poor* procedure because it slows up the work

73. Suppose that your supervisor has asked you to investigate some new gardening procedure and give him a written report with a recommendation whether the new procedure should be used in the Park Department. 73.____
It would probably be BEST for you to put your recommendation

A. any place in the report where you can fit it in without too much trouble
B. at the end of the report after you have given the facts of your investigation
C. in the middle of the report
D. on a separate attached sheet

74. Just before the end of a new assistant gardener's probationary period, his supervisor, the gardener, turned in a report to the foreman on the new employee's work and record during the probationary period. In his report, the gardener did not make any recommendation whether the new employee should be kept on after his probationary period. 74.____
The gardener's action was

A. *bad* because it is the gardener's responsibility to make a recommendation whether the new employee should be kept on after the probationary period
B. *good* because he should be impartial to all new employees
C. *bad* because the new employee will not know if he is going to be kept on the job or not
D. *good* because it is the job of *higher-ups* to decide if new employees should be kept on after the end of probation

75. Suppose that an assistant gardener whom you supervise has an accident on the job and is hurt. 75.____
In your written report of this accident to your own superior, it is LEAST important for you to include information about

A. the assistant gardener's attitude toward other employees
B. the tool used when the accident happened
C. what you plan to do to prevent such accidents in the future
D. when the accident happened

76. Your supervisor gives you a letter of complaint from a citizen and tells you to *look into this and get the facts.* It would be a good idea for you, as a FIRST step, to 76.____

A. interview the person who wrote the letter at his home
B. speak to the people in your department who have knowledge of the matter complained about

C. turn this over to one of your men who is not very busy
D. write the person a letter telling him that the matter he complains about is being looked into and will be settled to his satisfaction

77. If you are training a new member of your crew to use a piece of equipment, it would probably be LEAST important for you to 77.____

A. give him a set of written instructions on use of the equipment
B. give him an actual demonstration in using the equipment
C. watch him using the equipment the first time
D. check him frequently to see how he is progressing

78. Suppose that as a gardener you are in charge of several men. 78.____
Warning your men that they will be penalized if they do poor work is

A. *good* practice because it is only fair that they know what the penalties are for neglect of duty
B. *poor* practice because then you will actually have to penalize them if they don't do good work
C. *good* practice because they will try to do better work
D. *poor* practice because they should be encouraged to do good work without such warnings

79. A gardener supervising a group of men on a work project spoke to them one morning just before lunch about the importance of getting back to work on time after lunch. He turned to one of the men and said, *Bill, you have been particularly guilty of coming back late from lunch.* 79.____
The gardener's action was NOT good because

A. he could have taken care of the problem better and with less waste of time by issuing a written order to the men
B. he should have named at least one other man who was guilty of this violation
C. he should not have criticized one of his men in front of the other men
D. this was not a proper subject to talk about to his men at a group meeting

80. A gardener notices that one of his crew members does not get along with the rest of the crew. 80.____
The BEST thing for the gardener to do would be to

A. ignore the situation since it probably won't affect work output
B. tell his men they must get along with each other if they don't want to be transferred
C. try to find the reason for the trouble to see if the differences can be settled
D. write a report to his supervisor and await instructions

KEY (CORRECT ANSWERS)

1.	D	21.	C	41.	B	61.	B
2.	C	22.	A	42.	B	62.	C
3.	A	23.	D	43.	C	63.	A
4.	C	24.	C	44.	A	64.	B
5.	B	25.	C	45.	A	65.	B
6.	B	26.	C	46.	B	66.	A
7.	A	27.	D	47.	A	67.	B
8.	D	28.	D	48.	B	68.	C
9.	C	29.	D	49.	D	69.	D
10.	A	30.	B	50.	A	70.	D
11.	B	31.	C	51.	C	71.	B
12.	B	32.	C	52.	E	72.	C
13.	D	33.	A	53.	B	73.	B
14.	A	34.	A	54.	B	74.	A
15.	C	35.	A	55.	B	75.	A
16.	B	36.	B	56.	C	76.	B
17.	D	37.	B	57.	A	77.	A
18.	D	38.	C	58.	C	78.	D
19.	D	39.	A	59.	A	79.	C
20.	D	40.	A	60.	B	80.	C

EXAMINATION SECTION
TEST 1

DIRECTIONS: Each question or incomplete statement is followed by several suggested answers or completions. Select the one that BEST answers the question or completes the statement. *PRINT THE LETTER OF THE CORRECT ANSWER IN THE SPACE AT THE RIGHT.*

1. A herbicide is a chemical PRIMARILY used as a(n) 1.____

   A. disinfectant
   B. fertilizer
   C. insect killer
   D. weed killer

2. Established plants that continue to blossom year after year without reseeding are GENERALLY known as 2.____

   A. annuals
   B. parasites
   C. perennials
   D. symbiotics

3. A ferrous sulfate solution is sometimes used to treat shrubs or trees that have a deficiency of 3.____

   A. boron B. copper C. iron D. zinc

4. A tree is described as deciduous. This means PRIMARILY that it 4.____

   A. bears nuts instead of fruit
   B. has been pruned recently
   C. usually grows in swampy ground
   D. loses its leaves in the fall

5. If you are told that a container holds a 20-7-7 fertilizer, it is MOST likely that twenty percent of this fertilizer is 5.____

   A. nitrogen
   B. oxygen
   C. phosphoric acid
   D. potash

6. The landscape drawings for a school indicate the planting of *Acer platanoides* at a certain location on the grounds. Acer platanoides is a type of 6.____

   A. privet hedge
   B. rose bush
   C. maple tree
   D. tulip bed

7. The commercial fertilizer *5-10-5* refers to 5% ______, 10% ______, 5% ______. 7.____

   A. nitrogen; phosphoric acid; potash
   B. rotted manure; calcium chloride; bone meal
   C. soda; tobacco dust; bone meal
   D. tobacco dust; rotted manure; sulphur

8. The slope or slant of a soil line is 1/4" per foot.
   If this drainage line is 50' long, the difference in elevation from one end to the other is, in feet, MOST NEARLY 8.____

   A. 0.55 B. 1.04 C. 2.08 D. 12.5

9. The BEST method to use in watering trees and shrubs is to use 9.____

A. jet-type velocity at roots
B. hose with fine nozzle spray once a week and done well
C. a hose only when needed to soak roots
D. rotating single jet sprinkler

10. Little white insects that look like small shrimps and feed on the roots of grass are called 10.____

A. grubs
B. ricks
C. praying mantis
D. crabs

11. A term used to indicate a lawn chemical weed killer is 11.____

A. germicide
B. emulsified
C. herbicide
D. vitrified

12. The area of a lawn which is 58 feet wide by 96 feet long is MOST NEARLY _______ square feet. 12.____

A. 5000 B. 5500 C. 6000 D. 6500

13. If it is not possible to plant new shrubs immediately upon delivery in the spring, they should be stored in a(n) 13.____

A. sheltered outdoor area
B. unsheltered outdoor area
C. boiler room
D. warm place indoors

14. Peat moss is GENERALLY used for its 14.____

A. food value
B. nitrogen
C. alkalinity
D. moisture retaining quality

15. A checklist of outdoor tasks which should be performed in March and April should NOT include 15.____

A. fertilizing lawn areas
B. applying dormant spray
C. cleaning window wells
D. spraying broad-leaved weeds

16. Lawns should be mowed when the grass has attained a height of _______ inch(es) with the mower set at _______. inch(es). 16.____

A. 4; 3 B. 3; 2 C. 2; 1 D. 1; 1/2

17. The common name for a tree called Quercus Alba is 17.____

A. pine B. maple C. oak D. cedar

18. A tree which is considered to be suitable for street curb planting should 18.____

A. grow rapidly
B. have colorful foliage
C. be an evergreen
D. be straight and symmetrical

19. The component of fertilizers which aids in keeping grass from turning brown in the summer time is 19.____

A. limestone B. calcium C. chlordane D. nitrogen

20. A rectangular plot is 30 feet wide by 60 feet long. The length of the diagonal, in feet, is MOST NEARLY 20.____

A. 68 B. 67 C. 66 D. 65

21. Pruning of street trees is the responsibility of the 21.____

A. homeowners
B. lighting company
C. Department of Parks or Highways
D. sanitation department

22. Of the following, the one that is MOST likely to be used in landscaping work as ground cover is 22.____

A. Barberry B. Forsythia
C. Pachysandra D. Viburnum

23. To help plants survive the shock of transplanting, in most cases, it is BEST to 23.____

A. spray them with insecticide every day for a week
B. cover the foliage with burlap for a day or two
C. shade them from the sun for a week or two
D. prune them every day for a week or two

24. Garden soil which has a pH reading of 6.0 is said to be 24.____

A. neutral B. slightly acid
C. slightly alkaline D. strongly acid

25. Summer blooming flower bulbs should be stored in a ______ place. 25.____

A. warm, dry B. warm, moist
C. cool, moist D. cool, dry

26. The one of the following procedures which is NOT recommended for growing turfgrass in shaded areas is to 26.____

A. fertilize more frequently than normal
B. water deeply and frequently
C. compact the soil as much as possible
D. prune shallow tree roots as much as possible

27. Hedges should be trimmed so that the top is ______ than the bottom with the solid leaf growth starting ______. the ground. 27.____

A. *narrower,* about eighteen inches above
B. *narrower;* as close as possible to
C. *wider;* about eighteen inches above
D. *wider;* as close as possible to

28. When cutting a branch off a tree, it is DESIRABLE to undercut because it will 28.____

A. prevent the weight of the branch from tearing off bark and wood below the cut
B. make the tree grow stronger and straighter
C. let the saw work smoother and easier
D. make it easier to cut up the limb

29. The MAIN reason for applying lime to soil is to control its 29.____

A. aridity
B. fertilization
C. acidity
D. porosity

30. The GREATEST danger to a tree from a large unprotected wound is that 30.____

A. birds may build a nest in it
B. the tree may bleed to death
C. the wound may become infected
D. it is open to the elements

31. The fertilizer that is used for the care of trees should have a HIGH content of 31.____

A. DDT B. nitrogen C. sulphur D. carbon

32. The area of the plot shown at the right is ______ square feet. 32.____

A. 25,300
B. 26,700
C. 28,100
D. 30,500

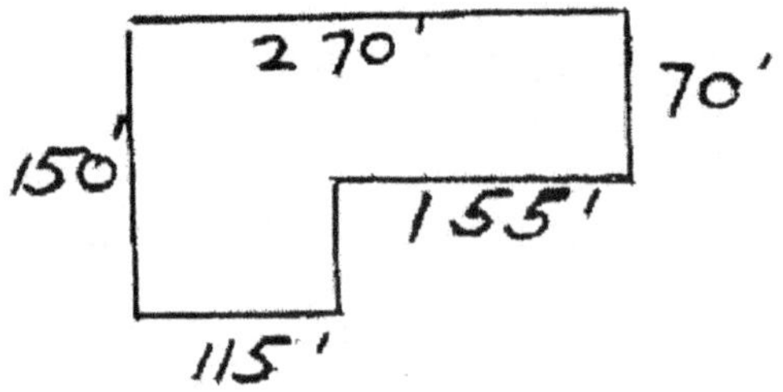

33. Before pruning a tree, the FIRST step should be to determine 33.____

A. if there is insect infestation
B. the general health of the tree
C. the desired results
D. amount of excess foliage

34. Under normal conditions during the growing season, lawns should receive a good saturation of water with a spray 34.____

A. once a day
B. once a week
C. once a month
D. twice a month

35. A pH value of 4 would indicate a(n)______solution. 35.____

A. acid B. neutral C. alkaline D. dry

KEY (CORRECT ANSWERS)

1. D
2. C
3. C
4. D
5. A
6. C
7. A
8. B
9. C
10. A
11. C
12. B
13. A
14. D
15. D
16. B
17. C
18. D
19. D
20. B
21. C
22. C
23. C
24. B
25. D
26. C
27. B
28. A
29. C
30. C
31. B
32. C
33. C
34. B
35. A

EXAMINATION SECTION
TEST 1

DIRECTIONS: Each question or incomplete statement is followed by several suggested answers or completions. Select the one that BEST answers the question or completes the statement. *PRINT THE LETTER OF THE CORRECT ANSWER IN THE SPACE AT THE RIGHT.*

1. Which of the following is an example of a perennial plant? 1.____

   A. Marigolds
   B. Purple cornflowers
   C. Cosmos
   D. Impatiens

2. When is the best time to prune flowering shrubs that bloom in the spring? 2.____

   A. In the spring before they bloom
   B. In the winter when they are dormant
   C. During the summer
   D. In the spring after they bloom

3. The term _____ refers to pollinated plant varieties that have been maintained by farmers and gardeners for several generations. 3.____

   A. heirloom
   B. cultivar
   C. hardy annual
   D. containerized

4. The removal of flowers as they fade is a practice known as 4.____

   A. topping
   B. hybridizing
   C. deadheading
   D. edging

5. Which of the following is a benefit of successional planting? 5.____

   A. It increases germination rates
   B. It provides continuous yield
   C. It reduces soil temperatures
   D. It improves irrigation

6. The percentage of N-P-K listed on the fertilizer label refers to the 6.____

   A. amount of nitrogen, phosphorus and potassium present in the fertilizer
   B. recommended rate of application
   C. soil cation balance
   D. amount of nitrogen, phosphorus and magnesium present in the fertilizer

7. pH is a measure of _____ in the soil. 7._____

A. moisture-holding capacity
B. nutrient cycling
C. temperature
D. acidity or alkalinity

8. Which of the following is an example of an herbaceous plant? 8._____

A. Tulip tree
B. Rose of Sharon
C. Coreopsis
D. Flowering quince

9. Which of the following insects is NOT considered beneficial to gardens? 9._____

A. Praying mantis B. Aphid C. Lady beetle D. Lacewing

10. In general, the yellowing of leaves can be attributed to 10._____

A. chlorosis
B. frost damage
C. drought
D. herbicide damage

11. Which of the following can be added to soil to promote better drainage? 11._____

A. Nitrogen
B. Sand
C. Clay
D. Silt

12. If a plant has hardiness zone of 5, in which of the following zones would it NOT survive? 12._____

A. Zone 9
B. Zone 7b
C. Zone 5
D. Zone 3

13. The difference between an annual plant and a biennial plant is that 13._____

A. an annual plant completes its lifecycle in one year and a biennial plant completes its lifecycle in two years
B. an annual plant flowers once a year and biennial plant flowers twice a year
C. an annual plant completes its lifecycle in two years and a biennial plant completes its lifecycle in one year
D. an annual plant flowers twice a year and a biennial plant flowers once a year

14. The purpose of staking a plant is to 14.____

A. kill the unwanted plant
B. fertilize the plant
C. provide structural support
D. inhibit the plant's growth

15. When is the best time to mow a lawn? 15.____

A. During the hottest part of the day
B. Directly after fertilization
C. When it is raining
D. During the coolest part of the day

16. Jim is choosing a plant to put beneath his maple tree in a spot that receives two hours of direct sunlight a day. Which of the following plants would be a good choice for Jim? 16.____

A. Hosta
B. Purple coneflower
C. Rose bush
D. Lilac bush

17. Which plant would NOT be appropriate to plant under a power line? 17.____

A. Ornamental grass
B. Oak tree
C. Rose bush
D. Hosta

18. Susan is preparing her garden for the new planting season by amending the soil with lime. The reason Susan is doing this is because she wants to 18.____

A. lower the pH of the soil
B. improve drainage
C. kill grubs and other pests living beneath the surface
D. raise the pH of the soil

19. Which of the following statements about groundcovers is true? 19.____

A. They only grow in shade
B. They are always deciduous
C. They can be woody or herbaceous
D. They only reach a mature height of one foot or less

20. Gardeners refer to compost as "black gold" because it 20.____

A. is one of the best soil conditioners available
B. eliminates weeds
C. compacts the soil
D. repels pests

21. What is the primary purpose of cold frames? 21.____

A. Moisture conservation
B. Temperature reduction
C. Season extension
D. Hybridization

22. One benefit of gardening in raised beds is that 22.____

A. they eliminate weeds
B. they conserve water
C. the soil stays cool longer in the fall
D. the soil warms up earlier in the spring

23. When selecting a fertilizer for your lawn, which mineral should be found in highest concentration? 23.____

A. Zinc
B. Nitrogen
C. Copper
D. Phosphorus

24. Tom plans to add bulbs to his garden next season. Which of the following plants and flowers should he consider growing? 24.____

I. Tulips
II. Daylilies
III. Sunflowers
IV. Elephant Ears

A. I and IV B. I and III C. II and III D. I, II and IV

25. When planting in a warm, dry area, a gardener should choose ____ because of their high heat tolerance. 25.____

A. pansies
B. snapdragons
C. sedums
D. primroses

KEY (CORRECT ANSWERS)

1. B	11. B	21. C
2. D	12. D	22. D
3. A	13. A	23. B
4. C	14. C	24. A
5. B	15. D	25. C
6. A	16. A	
7. D	17. B	
8. C	18. D	
9. B	19. C	
10. A	20. A	

TEST 2

DIRECTIONS: Each question or incomplete statement is followed by several suggested answers or completions. Select the one that BEST answers the question or completes the statement. *PRINT THE LETTER OF THE CORRECT ANSWER IN THE SPACE AT THE RIGHT.*

1. The ideal pH range for most plants is between 1.____

   A. 4.5 and 5.5
   B. 6.0 and 7.0
   C. 8.5 and 9.5
   D. 2.0 and 3.0

2. A shoot growing from the roots or base of another plant is called a 2.____

   A. sucker
   B. limb
   C. spur
   D. tendril

3. Which of the following is NOT a feature of organic gardening? 3.____

   A. Use of manures and fertilizers derived from plant or animal sources
   B. Encouragement of biodiversity
   C. Efforts to conserve resources, like saving and storing water
   D. Application of synthetically produced pesticides and fertilizers

4. Ryan is trying to avoid the use of peat-moss potting mixes because he has heard that the extraction of peat moss is damaging to the environment. Which of the following would be a good alternative to peat-based products? 4.____

   A. Leaf mold
   B. Nitrogen
   C. Fish meal
   D. Kelp

5. Trees that do not exceed a height of _____ feet are the most appropriate choice for small yards. 5.____

   A. 40 B. 20 C. 50 D. 10

6. Which of the following is an example of an evergreen? 6.____

   A. Dogwood
   B. Birch
   C. Juniper
   D. Box elder

7. Vertical gardening is a technique that uses 7._____

   A. numerous weeping plant varieties to create a vertical aesthetic in your garden
   B. hanging baskets for starting plants to save space before moving them to multilayered raised beds
   C. plants to provide a privacy barrier along property edges
   D. wall spaces on houses, garages or other buildings to grow plants

8. Which of the following trees would be a good choice for an urban area because of its high pollution tolerance? 8._____

   A. Red maple
   B. Sugar maple
   C. Ginkgo biloba
   D. White oak

9. Which of the following pests is most likely to affect shrubs? 9._____

   A. Parasitoid wasps
   B. Spider mites
   C. Millipedes
   D. Pollen beetles

10. Lance is looking for a tree that will provide his yard with visual interest in both the fall and the spring. Which tree should Lance plant? 10._____

   A. Juneberry
   B. Box elder
   C. Silver maple
   D. Black gum

11. When is the best time to prune shrubs that bloom in the summer or fall? 11._____

   A. In the summer or fall just after they bloom
   B. Early spring
   C. Early winter
   D. In the summer or fall just before they bloom

12. Pruning cuts that remove an entire branch or limb are known as _____ cuts. 12._____

   A. pinching B. shearing C. heading D. thinning

13. The best way to keep rabbits out of your garden is to 13._____

   A. spray castor oil on your plants
   B. lay chunky bark mulch or ornamental rocks on your soil
   C. put up a fence that extends underground
   D. spread shredded lemon of grapefruit peels around your garden

14. Abnormal lumps that appear on leaves, stems and branches are known as 14._____

A. tumors
B. suckers
C. galls
D. blight

15. Which of the following is NOT a method of plant propagation? 15._____

A. Taking cuttings
B. Dividing roots
C. Transplanting
D. Air layering

16. Which of the following plants is known for its ability to attract beneficial insects to your garden? 16._____

A. Goldenrod
B. Ash tree
C. Hosta
D. Blue fescue

17. Which of the following is NOT a feature of a bulb? 17._____

A. They have a basal plate
B. They have no tunic
C. They have rings called scales
D. They form new bulbs known as offsets

18. Janice is considering moving to a climate with a very long growing season. Which of the following plant hardiness zones would be best for her? 18._____

A. 2 B. 9 C. 4 D. 5

19. Which of the following perennials does NOT tolerate division? 19._____

A. Hosta
B. Feather reed grass
C. Switchgrass
D. Lupine

20. Which plant is most likely to produce seed in its first year? 20._____

A. Cosmos
B. Columbine
C. Queen Anne's lace
D. Hollyhock

21. Which of the following plants is in the Fabaceae family? 21._____

A. Cosmos
B. Eastern redbud
C. Hosta
D. Hollyhock

22. Gardeners use rain barrels in order to 22._____

A. conserve water
B. release water at regulated times
C. prevent water from flooding your garden
D. trap insects

23. Peter is growing tomato and pepper seedlings indoors and has gradually acclimated the plants to outside conditions. This process is known as 23._____

A. letting out
B. girdling
C. grafting
D. hardening off

24. Which type of fungus is a common problem for seedlings? 24._____

A. Shoestring root rot
B. Conk
C. Damping off
D. Canker

25. Tandy wants to plant a shrub outside of her window that will have a pleasant scent in the late winter and early spring. Which plant would be a good choice for Tandy? 25._____

A. Winterberry
B. Holly
C. Wintersweet
D. Summersweet

KEY (CORRECT ANSWERS)

1. B	11. B	21. B
2. A	12. D	22. A
3. D	13. C	23. D
4. A	14. C	24. C
5. B	15. C	25. C
6. C	16. A	
7. D	17. B	
8. C	18. B	
9. B	19. D	
10. A	20. A	

TEST 3

DIRECTIONS: Each question or incomplete statement is followed by several suggested answers or completions. Select the one that BEST answers the question or completes the statement. *PRINT THE LETTER OF THE CORRECT ANSWER IN THE SPACE AT THE RIGHT.*

1. When is the best time to prune formal hedges? 1._____

   A. Early spring
   B. Late winter
   C. Late summer
   D. Late spring

2. Soil with a pH of 4.5 is considered 2._____

   A. strongly acidic
   B. strongly alkaline
   C. neutral
   D. mildly alkaline

3. The term _____ refers to the configuration of sand, silt and clay particles in the soil. 3._____

   A. alkalinity
   B. percolation
   C. soil structure
   D. topsoil

4. Annabelle needs to raise the soil pH in her garden. Which of the following amendments should she add to her soil to make it less acidic? 4._____

   A. Sulfur B. Nitrogen C. Peat moss D. Lime

5. What is the difference between single digging and double digging? 5._____

   A. Single digging involves digging deeper into the soil than double digging.
   B. Double digging involves the use of a spade whereas single digging involves the use of a trowel.
   C. Double digging involves digging deeper into the soil than single digging.
   D. Single digging involves the use of a spade whereas double digging involves the use of a trowel.

6. A cactus is an example of a(n) _____ plant. 6._____

   A. deciduous
   B. succulent
   C. coniferous
   D. annual

7. _____ is the uppermost layer of soil and is usually very fertile. 7._____

A. Topsoil
B. Mulch
C. Compost
D. Peat moss

8. Which of the following USDA plant hardiness zones is vulnerable to frost at any time of the year? 8._____

A. 12 B. 1 C. 5 D. 0

9. Lucas has noticed that the flowers on his perennials have begun to turn brown. In addition, the leaves are mottled, with some silver streaks. Lucas's perennials are most likely infested with 9._____

A. powdery mildew
B. weevils
C. thrips
D. coral spot

10. Picotee flower is a flower 10._____

A. whose edge is a different color than the rest of the petal
B. with extra petals
C. shaped like a star
D. with three different color petals

11. Joni lives in a heavily forested area that receives very little sun and she is looking for a perennial to plant in her yard. Which of the following perennials would be a good choice for Joni? 11._____

A. Common yarrow
B. Purple coneflower
C. Bee balm
D. Lady's mantle

12. Which of the following is an example of a perennial weed? 12._____

A. Common chickweed
B. Annual bluegrass
C. Dandelion
D. Dwarf nettle

13. Which of the following is true of sandy soil? 13._____

A. It retains nutrients longer
B. It dries out quickly
C. It requires less frequent applications of fertilizer
D. It retains too much moisture

14. Which of the following is considered the ideal soil texture? 14._____

A. Loam B. Clay C. Sand D. Silt

15. The scientific or botanical names of plants consist of several parts. Which of the following make up the plant names? 15._____

I. Class
II. Genus
III. Order
IV. Specific epithet

A. I and III B. II and IV C. I and IV D. I, II and III

16. Which of the following is NOT a type of plant stem? 16._____

A. Herbaceous stems
B. Woody stems
C. Bulbs
D. Pinnate stems

17. Nelly has purchased a few plants that are not very hardy and she wants to do everything she can to reduce their risk of winter damage. To give them the least temperature variation and the greatest chance of survival, Nelly should put these plants on the ______ side of her house. 17._____

A. south B. north C. southwest D. west

18. What is the primary purpose of a tiller? 18._____

A. Compact the soil
B. Deter pests
C. Hold in moisture
D. Churn up the soil

19. Which of the following nutrients is considered a secondary nutrient, meaning that it is important for plant survival but not as important as a primary nutrient? 19._____

A. Calcium
B. Nitrogen
C. Phosphorus
D. Potassium

20. Which of the following nutrients is considered a micronutrient, meaning that plants only need it in extremely low doses? 20._____

A. Magnesium
B. Potassium
C. Copper
D. Sulfur

21. Which of the following is NOT a common goal of mulching? 21._____

A. Weed prevention
B. Pest prevention
C. Moisture retention
D. Beautification

22. When pruning trees and shrubs, you should do all of the following EXCEPT 22._____

A. remove dead wood
B. prune in the winter to stimulate new shoots
C. remove diseased wood
D. use only heading cuts

23. Which of the following plants can be propagated from stem cuttings? 23._____

A. Fuchsia
B. Cosmos
C. Pansy
D. Verbena

24. Sarah has noticed that her arborvitae trees are suddenly covered with cylindrical cones. Sarah is certain that this is not a normal part of the trees' growth. What pest has infested Sarah's arborvitaes? 24._____

A. Aphids
B. Borers
C. Bagworm
D. Chinch bugs

25. Which of the following creatures do NOT cause damage to plants once they have reached adulthood? 25._____

A. Mice
B. Moles
C. Gophers
D. Moths

KEY (CORRECT ANSWERS)

1. D	11. D	21. B
2. A	12. C	22. D
3. C	13. B	23. A
4. D	14. A	24. C
5. C	15. B	25. D
6. B	16. D	
7. A	17. B	
8. B	18. D	
9. C	19. A	
10. A	20. C	

TEST 4

DIRECTIONS: Each question or incomplete statement is followed by several suggested answers or completions. Select the one that BEST answers the question or completes the statement. *PRINT THE LETTER OF THE CORRECT ANSWER IN THE SPACE AT THE RIGHT.*

1. What is one of the primary goals of crop rotation? 1.____

   A. Lengthen the growing season
   B. Speed up harvest time
   C. Ensure equal water distribution
   D. Prevent pests and diseases

2. A green manure crop is one that 2.____

   A. is grown in order to improve soil conditions
   B. can be harvested in both the spring and the fall
   C. requires no fertilization or maintenance
   D. produces an unusually high yield

3. Which of the following is NOT a disease that affects herbs? 3.____

   A. Bacterial wilt
   B. Crown rot
   C. Red thread
   D. Powdery mildew

4. Which of the following statements about herb gardening is true? 4.____

   A. Herbs are more affected by pests and diseases than other garden plants
   B. You should harvest different parts of your herbs at different times of the year
   C. Herb gardens serve a purely decorative function
   D. Herbs require less moisture than other garden plants

5. Toni is looking for an annual with colorful foliage to plant in one of her new beds. Which of the following would be a good choice for Toni? 5.____

   A. Love-lies-bleeding
   B. Morning glory
   C. Lupine
   D. Bleeding heart

6. A raised bed that is not surrounded by a wall is known as a 6.____

   A. box B. berm C. hardscape D. range

7. The term _____ is used to describe a long, narrow planting bed along the edge of a garden or walkway. 7._____

A. island
B. berm
C. thatch
D. border

8. Which of the following is NOT considered a hardscape element of your garden? 8._____

A. Trellis
B. Walkway
C. Herbaceous border
D. Statue

9. Which of the following is an example of an environmental plant disease? 9._____

A. Aphids
B. Bacterial rot
C. Powdery mildew
D. Nitrogen deficiency

10. Pruning pine trees is best performed in 10._____

A. late spring
B. early fall
C. late winter
D. late summer

11. Which of the following is NOT a type of organic fertilizer? 11._____

A. Humus
B. Blood meal
C. Granular fertilizer
D. Epsom salt

12. A soil with a pH of 9.5 is 12._____

A. neutral
B. strongly alkaline
C. strongly acidic
D. mildly acidic

13. What is the ideal composition of loam soil? 13._____

A. 50% sand and 50% silt
B. 80% sand, 10% silt and 10% clay
C. 80% silt, 10% sand and 10% clay
D. 40% sand, 40% silt and 20% clay

14. Marcie has noticed that an animal has chewed the bark off around the entire circumference of one of her trees, and the part of the tree above the damage appears to be dying. This is an example of 14._____

A. dampening off
B. girdling
C. hardening off
D. wilting

15. In the winter, wide temperature fluctuations can cause plant roots to come out of the soil. This is known as 15._____

A. heaving B. girdling
C. wilting D. dampening

16. The term *growing season* refers to the 16._____

A. average number of days between the last frost of a year and the first frost of the subsequent year
B. average number of days that receive full sun annually
C. ratio of sunny to rainy days annually
D. average number of days between the first and last frost of the year

17. According to the American Horticultural Society, most plants begin to suffer heat-related damage at temperatures of _____ or higher. 17._____

A. 70°F B. 96°F C. 86°F D. 102°F

18. Manny has noticed that the leaves on his sunflowers have reddish-brown marks on them, and many of the leaves have dropped. Manny's sunflowers are most likely affected by 18._____

A. root rot B. downy mildew
C. rust D. bacterial wilt

19. How many hours of direct sunlight do most vegetables require? 19._____

A. 2 B. 6 C. 10 D. 12

20. Which of the following is an example of a cultivar? 20._____

A. Eastern redbud
B. Pale purple coneflower
C. False sunflower
D. Bloodgood Japanese maple

21. Which of the following parts of a plant CANNOT be used for a cutting? 21._____

A. flowers B. stems
C. roots D. leaves

22. What is vegetative propagation? 22._____

A. Reproduction without sex
B. Reproduction between perennials
C. Insect pollination
D. Wind pollination

23. During the winter, perennials in cold climates enter into a period known as 23._____

A. reproduction
B. dormancy
C. necrosis
D. wilt

24. Which of the following is NOT a monocot? 24._____

A. Lilies
B. Daffodils
C. Thistle
D. Irises

25. Which of the following trees is both deciduous and coniferous? 25._____

A. White oak
B. Silver maple
C. Honey locust
D. Gingko biloba

KEY (CORRECT ANSWERS)

1. D	11. C	21. A
2. A	12. B	22. A
3. C	13. D	23. B
4. B	14. B	24. C
5. A	15. A	25. D
6. B	16. D	
7. D	17. C	
8. C	18. C	
9. D	19. B	
10. A	20. D	

READING COMPREHENSION
UNDERSTANDING AND INTERPRETING WRITTEN MATERIAL
EXAMINATION SECTION
TEST 1

DIRECTIONS: Each question consists of a statement. You are to indicate whether the statement is TRUE (T) or FALSE (F). *PRINT THE LETTER OF THE CORRECT ANSWER IN THE SPACE AT THE RIGHT.*

Questions 1-3.

DIRECTIONS: Questions 1 through 3 are to be answered based ONLY on information given in the following paragraph and not upon any other information you may have.

The belt should always be taut when clutch is fully engaged and at no other time. To check the belt for proper tension, first start the engine, and then bear down lightly on the handle of the mower in order to raise the mower wheels off the ground. While in this position, engage the clutch; then stop the engine by shorting the sparkplug with the stop switch, leaving the clutch engaged. If the belt is not taut, loosen the nut which holds the countershaft pedestal in order to make the countershaft pedestal movable. Then slide the countershaft pedestal to the back to tighten the belt. Sliding the countershaft pedestal forward loosens the belt.

1. The only time the belt should be tight is when the clutch is engaged completely. 1.____

2. In testing the belt for correct tension, the clutch should be engaged after the mower wheels are raised off the ground. 2.____

3. To make the belt looser, tighten the nut holding the countershaft pedestal. 3.____

Questions 4-10.

DIRECTIONS: Questions 4 through 10 are to be answered based ONLY on information given in the following paragraph and not upon any other information you may have.

The soil around actively growing delphiniums should receive a thorough soaking at least once a week. Delphiniums can be transplanted either in the autumn or in the spring. The fine and fibrous root system of these plants facilitates their removal. Since delphiniums are among the first herbaceous plants to start growth in the spring, autumn transplanting is generally recommended because the plants then undoubtedly suffer less shock. If the work is done with extreme care, it is possible to move quite large plants when they are just coming into bloom. Large plants must be lifted with a generous quantity of earth in order that the root system remain intact. The use of a plastic spray will prevent wilting if applied before the plants are moved.

4. Delphiniums must be watered more than once a week. 4.____

5. Delphiniums are difficult to remove because of their thick, tough roots. 5.____

6. Delphiniums start growth earlier in the spring than many other herbaceous plants. 6.____

7. Delphiniums experience more shock from transplanting in the spring than in the fall. 7.____

8. To keep the root system together when large delphiniums are moved, a large amount of earth should be taken up with the roots. 8.____

9. One way of preventing a delphinium from wilting when moved is to apply a plastic spray to the plant beforehand. 9.____

10. Large delphinium plants are MOST easily moved at the time they are beginning to bloom. 10.____

Questions 11-15.

DIRECTIONS: Questions 11 through 15 are to be answered based ONLY on information given in the following paragraph and not upon any other information you may have.

To insure thick growth from the ground up, hedges should be cut back to a few inches from the ground when planted. The properly shaped hedge is narrower at the top than at the bottom, and the top should be rounded rather than flat. The sloping sides admit much light to the lower branches. A somewhat narrow and rounded top also sheds snow instead of accumulating a heavy load and sometimes bending or breaking under it.

11. Hedges should be cut down to a few inches from the ground after they have grown dense at the bottom. 11.____

12. Trimming of hedges should be done in such a way as to give them a rounded top. 12.____

13. A hedge shaped wider at the top than at the bottom will admit much light to the bottom branches. 13.____

14. Snow will tend to accumulate and stay on a hedge with a wide, flat top. 14.____

15. A hedge can sometimes be broken by the weight of the snow accumulated on top of it. 15.____

Questions 16-25.

DIRECTIONS: Questions 16 through 25 are to be answered based ONLY on information given in the following paragraph and not upon any other information you may have.

Arsenate of lead, the best known and most widely used stomach poison, comes in two forms, basic and acid. The basic form is less likely to burn tender growth but stays in suspension poorly and kills insects more slowly. Most commercial preparations are the acid form usually sold as a powder, sometimes as a paste. For general spraying, use the powder at the rate of 3 lbs. to 100 gallons of water; or in small quantities, use one heaping tablespoon to one gallon of water. If the paste form is available, use twice the amount recommended.

16. There is an acid form of arsenate of lead and a basic form of arsenate of lead. 16.____

17. No stomach poison is better known than arsenate of lead. 17.____

18. No other stomach poison is used as much as arsenate of lead. 18.____

19. The basic form of arsenate of lead kills insects more quickly than the acid form. 19.____

20. There are many forms of arsenate of lead. 20.____

21. The basic form of arsenate of lead is MORE likely to burn plants than the acid form. 21.____

22. The acid form of arsenate of lead is USUALLY sold as a paste. 22.____

23. Commercially prepared arsenate of lead is USUALLY of the acid form. 23.____

24. The paste of the acid form of arsenate of lead, when used for general spraying, should be mixed at the rate of 3 lbs. to 100 gallons of water. 24.____

25. The powder of the acid form of arsenate of lead, when used for general spraying, should be used at the rate of one heaping teaspoon to a gallon of water. 25.____

KEY (CORRECT ANSWERS)

1.	T	11.	F
2.	T	12.	T
3.	F	13.	F
4.	F	14.	T
5.	F	15.	T
6.	T	16.	T
7.	T	17.	T
8.	T	18.	T
9.	T	19.	F
10.	F	20.	F

21.	F
22.	F
23.	T
24.	F
25.	F

TEST 2

DIRECTIONS: Each question consists of a statement. You are to indicate whether the statement is TRUE (T) or FALSE (F). *PRINT THE LETTER OF THE CORRECT ANSWER IN THE SPACE AT THE RIGHT.*

Questions 1-9.

DIRECTIONS: Questions 1 through 9 are to be answered SOLELY on the basis of the information contained in the following passage and not upon any other information you may have.

Insecticides kill insects by poisoning, suffocation, or paralysis. They are grouped into three classes: stomach poisons, contact poisons, and fumigants. Fumigants are the most effective type to use when the insects are in a greenhouse or other enclosure. Occasionally, they are used in the open under tents placed over the plant. Commonly used fumigants are nicotine and carbon bisulphide. Stomach poisons are used against insects with biting and chewing mouth parts, such as beetles and caterpillars. There are two types of stomach poisons, poison baits and protectants. The most widely used stomach poisons are composed of some form of arsenic.

1. Nicotine is used as a stomach poison. 1.___
2. Fumigants are best to use on plants growing outdoors. 2.___
3. An insecticide kills insects in one of three ways. 3.___
4. When fumigants are used outdoors, the plant is covered with a tent. 4.___
5. A protectant is another name for a fumigant. 5.___
6. Beetles have the same kind of mouth parts as caterpillars. 6.___
7. Most contact poisons contain arsenic. 7.___
8. Carbon bisulphide is used against beetles and caterpillars. 8.___
9. A protectant is a type of stomach poison. 9.___

Questions 10-19.

DIRECTIONS: Questions 10 through 19 are to be answered SOLELY on the basis of the information contained in the following passage and not upon any other information you may have.

The Japanese beetle is nearly a half inch long, is bright shining green with bronze or reddish wing covers. There are five white spots made of tufts of white hairs along the sides of the abdomen and two distinct white spots at the tip of the abdomen below the tips of the wing covers. The larva is a white grub resembling that of the common May beetle or June bug, but only about half as big. The beetles begin to emerge from the soil the latter part of June and may be present until the first of October, but the period of greatest density lasts only from the middle of July to early August. The eggs, laid in the soil chiefly during July and August, hatch in 12 days, and the grubs soon begin to feed on grass roots near the surface. Toward the winter, they move downward about a foot to hibernate.

10. The larva of the June bug is half as large as the larva of the Japanese beetle. 10.____

11. The Japanese beetle has seven white spots on its abdomen. 11.____

12. The grubs of the Japanese beetle come up to the surface right after they hatch in order to feed on the grass. 12.____

13. The Japanese beetle is reddish bronze in color. 13.____

14. The Japanese beetles begin to come out of the soil after June. 14.____

15. The larva of the May beetle resembles the larva of the Japanese beetle. 15.____

16. The Japanese beetle ranges in size from 1/4 to 3/4 of an inch. 16.____

17. During the winter, Japanese beetle grubs live about a foot underground. 17.____

18. Japanese beetles are most plentiful from about July 15 to about August 10th. 18.____

19. The Japanese beetle lays its eggs in the ground. 19.____

Questions 20-25.

DIRECTIONS: Questions 20 through 25 are to be answered SOLELY on the basis of the information given in the following passage and not upon any other information you may have.

Lawnmowers as well as lawns suffer when the grass is cut too short. There is much more dust and dirt on the base of the blades of grass, near the soil, than there is higher up. This grit wears away the blades and the strike bar and quickly dulls them. Other bad practices are leaving the mower out overnight and failing to wipe the cutting edges dry after each mowing. A couple of dewy nights, a session with wet grass, and the sharp edge has rusted. The simple measure of wiping an oily rag across the edges of the blades and the cutting bar will prevent rusting of these important surfaces.

20. When the grass is cut too short, the lawnmower suffers. 20.____

21. There is more dirt on the base of a blade of grass than there is higher up. 21.____

22. The blades and the strike bar of a lawnmower are sharpened by the grit of the soil. 22.____

23. It is bad practice to leave the mower out overnight. 23.____

24. After each mowing, the cutting edges of a mower should be wiped dry. 24.____

25. Wiping the edges of the blades and the cutting bar with an oily rag will NOT prevent rusting. 25.____

KEY (CORRECT ANSWERS)

1. F
2. F
3. T
4. T
5. F
6. T
7. F
8. F
9. T
10. F
11. T
12. F
13. F
14. F
15. T
16. F
17. T
18. T
19. T
20. T
21. T
22. F
23. T
24. T
25. F

TEST 3

DIRECTIONS: Each question consists of a statement. You are to indicate whether the statement is TRUE (T) or FALSE (F). *PRINT THE LETTER OF THE CORRECT ANSWER IN THE SPACE AT THE RIGHT.*

Questions 1-10.

DIRECTIONS: Questions 1 through 10 are to be answered ONLY on the basis of the information given in the following paragraph and NOT upon any other information you may have.

A commercial fertilizer may be a single substance such as nitrate of soda, or it may be a combination of such materials which contains a definite ratio of the three main plant-food elements, nitrogen, phosphorus, and potassium. Such a mixture is said to be complete. And if the proportions of the three elements are such as to meet the full needs of a certain plant, the fertilizer is said to be balanced as well as complete. As the plant food compounds in commercial fertilizers are in highly soluble form, they should not be applied too heavily nor allowed to come in contact with plant parts. Small frequent applications are safest and least wasteful as they give less chance for the soluble salts to be dissolved and leached out of the soil before the plant roots can get them. It is usually advisable to water the soil after adding commercial fertilizer, both to put the fertilizer in solution so that the plants can take it up and to prevent the fertilizer from absorbing the moisture in the soil.

1. All commercial fertilizers consist of a combination of the three main plant food elements. 1.____
2. Nitrate of soda is available as a commercial fertilizer. 2.____
3. The three main plant food elements are nitrate of soda, nitrogen, and phosphorus. 3.____
4. A complete fertilizer contains nitrogen, potassium, and phosphorus. 4.____
5. Any fertilizer which contains nitrogen, potassium, and phosphorus is said to be balanced. 5.____
6. The plant food elements in commercial fertilizers are very soluble. 6.____
7. A commercial fertilizer should be mixed right in among the roots of a plant so that it becomes available quickly. 7.____
8. Commercial fertilizers should be applied to the soil in large amounts. 8.____
9. Commercial fertilizers must be in solution before it can be taken up by plants. 9.____
10. If the soil is not watered when commercial fertilizer is applied, the fertilizer may absorb the moisture that is already in the soil. 10.____

Questions 11-25.

DIRECTIONS: Questions 11 through 25 are to be answered ONLY on the basis of the information given in the following paragraph and NOT upon any other information you may have.

Bent grass is the common name for Agrostis, a large class of mostly low-growing and spreading grasses including some valuable, high-class lawn grasses as well as the important pasture grass, Redtop. Bent grasses are annual or perennial, have somewhat rough, flat or slightly rolled leaves, and bear loose panicles of small reddish flowers. While some of the forms are grown from seed, those used for fine lawns and golf courses are of the creeping type and are increasingly being grown from stolons, which are simply the chopped-up stems. Bent grasses will do well in sun or partial shade, but are not in any sense a shady-spot variety. The soil should be well supplied with thoroughly rotted manure and receive a good application of a balanced complete fertilizer before planting time. In sowing, use about one pound of seed to 250 square feet; if stolons are used, broadcast them at the rate of 25 square feet of stolons to 200 square feet of area. They must then be covered lightly with soil, rotted and watered.

11. Agrostis is the common name for Bent grass. 11.____

12. Redtop is a pasture grass. 12.____

13. Agrostis is a variety of Redtop. 13.____

14. Most Bent grasses are low-growing. 14.____

15. Not all Bent grasses are perennial. 15.____

16. All Bent grasses are annual. 16.____

17. Bent grasses bear flowers. 17.____

18. Creeping Bent grasses are used from seed. 18.____

19. A stolon is a chopped-up Bent grass seed. 19.____

20. Bent grasses are good for planting in heavily shaded areas. 20.____

21. Before Bent grass is planted, rotted manure and a balanced complete fertilizer should be added to the soil. 21.____

22. Bent grass may be sown at the rate of 1/2 pound of seed to 125 square feet. 22.____

23. When Bent grass is planted by means of stolons, 25 pounds of stolons should be broadcast to 200 square feet of area. 23.____

24. After being broadcast, stolons should be covered with at least three inches of soil. 24.____

25. In sowing, the ratio of pounds of seed to square foot coverage is approximately 1 to 25. 25.____

KEY (CORRECT ANSWERS)

1. F
2. T
3. F
4. T
5. F
6. T
7. F
8. F
9. T
10. T
11. F
12. T
13. F
14. T
15. T
16. F
17. T
18. T
19. F
20. F
21. T
22. T
23. F
24. F
25. F

CONTENTS

Introduction 2

New Lawn Establishment 3
Site considerations 3
Planting 6
Postplanting care 10

Routine Lawn Maintenance 11
Mowing 11
Fertilizing 12
Watering 17
Rolling 18
Topdressing 18
Thatch 18
Lawn maintenance calendar 20

Lawn Pests 24
Weeds 24
Diseases 28
Insects 34

Special Lawn Problems 36
Improving a poor lawn 36
Renovating a poor lawn 36
Lawns in the shade 37
Steep slopes 37
Turfgrasses and substitutes to avoid 37
Moss 38
Moles, skunks, and other animals 38

Appendix 39
Calculations for home lawn practices 39
Directions for soil sampling 40

INTRODUCTION

Lawns play a significant role in the residential landscape. Of the 30 million acres of land in New York State, approximately 1.2 million acres are maintained under turfgrass conditions. About three-quarters of this amount is devoted to the residential lawn.

Lawns can provide many benefits if properly established and maintained. Turfgrass enhances our environment by filtering out atmospheric pollutants; cooling the air as it gives off water, an important process in highly urbanized areas; improving the structure of soils by adding organic matter; eliminating soil erosion; and reducing noise pollution when used in conjunction with physical barriers.

Lawns provide an attractive, inexpensive ground cover especially in the harsh conditions of full sun. In addition, a well-maintained landscape greatly increases the value of property. Turfgrass is the only suitable living surface that can be used repeatedly for recreational purposes. Many individuals take great pride in the appearance of their lawns and derive enjoyment in caring for them.

The information needed to establish and maintain an acceptable lawn is presented in this publication and is divided into four major sections: "New Lawn Establishment," "Routine Lawn Maintenance," "Lawn Pests," and "Special Lawn Problems." If you are planning to establish a lawn, you should read the entire bulletin. If you have a special concern, review the information in the most appropriate section.

Site Considerations

Survey the conditions on your property to determine if turfgrass is the most suitable ground cover. Not all residential sites have the most favorable conditions for growing an acceptable lawn. Heavily shaded areas and severely sloped areas are not ideal locations for lawns. Such areas are difficult to establish and maintain and have proved to be very costly.

Site Preparation

Taking the time to carefully prepare your new area will help ensure a successful lawn. Many future lawn problems can be avoided by following the simple procedures outlined.

Control Perennial Grassy Weeds

Certain weeds are impossible to control without killing the lawn. It is important to remove these weeds before establishment. The most troublesome weeds of this type are quackgrass, yellow nutsedge, and creeping bentgrass as well as other coarse pasture-type grasses. A non-selective herbicide should be used in controlling these weeds

Drainage

Unless excess water drains rapidly through the soil, the turfgrass will have a poor root system and weak growth. If your soil stays wet after a heavy rain, you cannot grow a satisfactory lawn until you provide supplemental drainage.

Grading

For a new home, the house foundation and the curb or sidewalk level are the fixed grade points. An older property has more places that cannot be changed. The problem in grading is to arrange the soil between these fixed points in gradual, pleasant slopes to direct water away from the house and off the property.

Avoid sudden steep slopes because they are hard to establish and difficult to maintain. Where much soil must be changed, move the topsoil into a pile and rearrange the subsoil to the desired grade or slope. Then spread the topsoil evenly over the subsoil. In grading, be sure to allow for the gradual settling of loose soil. A 6-inch layer of loose soil settles to about 5 inches. It is better to prepare the seedbed several weeks before the planting time, to allow the loose soil to settle enough to make the final grading easy. Also, you can destroy any weeds that come up.

However, if the best planting time arrives by the time you begin to work, go ahead with the planting.

Soil

Topsoil

If you are building a new home, be sure to see that the topsoil is scraped into a pile and saved for even distribution after the builder has finished and the rough grading has been done. This important point is often overlooked, and only subsoil remains. If you do not have all or most of the original topsoil, plan to add at least 4 to 6 inches of good topsoil, even though it is expensive. This is the surest, and often the most economical, way to produce a good lawn.

Acquiring a good topsoil is often difficult; therefore, you should seek advice from your Cooperative Extension agent. Bring in a representative sample of the soils you are considering buying for an evaluation of soil pH, nutrient level, and physical condition. In many cases the top 6 inches of a farm pasture or cropland soil is very desirable for lawn use. One word of caution: Find out if any herbicides have been used on this land because some are harmful to turfgrass. Do not accept river bottom silt, soil dug from a hill with a power shovel, or factory waste, regardless of how "rich" any of this material looks. If you live near a large city or in some other area where good topsoil is not available, work with what you have.

Table 1. Amount of ground limestone needed to raise soil pH in upper 4″–6″ of soil

Raising pH to 6.5*	Pounds of limestone/1,000 sq ft of area		
Original pH	**Sandy**	**Loamy**	**Clayey**
5.5	45	60	100
5.0	70	90	150
4.5	80	100	180
4.0	100	160	200

*These rates cannot be used on established turfgrass.
See lawn maintenance section for rates on established turfgrass.

Even poor soils, if well drained, often can produce a fairly good lawn with proper soil preparation, adequate fertilization, and the right kind of turfgrass seed at the proper season.
Then, if the lawn can be maintained for a few years with adequate water and fertilizer added, the turfgrass will produce enough organic matter to improve the soil gradually. One must be patient when trying to improve poor soils; it may take several years to produce an acceptable lawn.

Soil texture and organic matter

A very sandy soil is too "light or open" in texture. It is like a mass of tiny stones, with too few smaller bits of soil between the sand grains to hold water and fertilizer materials. Turfgrass does not do its best when water and nutrients are lacking. To improve a very sandy soil, work about 1–2 inches of organic matter into the surface 4–6 inches of soil. Another method involves thoroughly mixing 1 inch of heavier soil with the top 4 inches of sand. A sandy soil is improved more if you add both organic matter and heavier soil than if you add either material alone.

A clay soil is a "heavy or dense soil." It is slippery and sticky when wet and shrinks and cracks open as it dries. Turfgrass cannot do its best in heavy clay, for there is not enough air in the soil for good root growth. Heavy traffic from people walking or playing packs a clay soil even more tightly. Work organic matter into a heavy clay soil to improve it. Do not work sand into a clay soil; it will pack harder than before and become much like concrete.

If your soil needs organic matter, any one of several materials will do a good job. *Avoid* using wood chips, shavings, or sawdust since they can "steal" nitrogen, which is vital to the turf, from the soil. For each 1,000 square feet of new lawn, use 4 large (6-cubic-foot) bales of peat or from 2 to 3 cubic yards of well-rotted manure or cultivated peat or 3 to 4 cubic yards of spent mushroom soil. Smaller amounts of organic matter are of little value. Sewage sludge is sometimes available from your local sewage treatment plant. It can be used fairly successfully if it does not contain excessive amounts of heavy metals from industrial wastes.

Cover crops and green-manure crops are not practical for lawns, because the amount of organic matter they add is relatively small and is not worth the cost, effort, and inconvenience.

Lime or sulfur

Some soils are too acid or too alkaline to grow good turfgrass. The best time to correct the soil pH is before planting. First, determine if your soil is too acid or alkaline by having the soil tested. The results of the soil test are reported in terms of pH units.[1] The ordinary range for New York soils is from 4.5 (acid) to pH 7.8 (alkaline). It is desirable to have your soil in the pH range from 6.0 to 7.0. Most Cooperative Extension offices can test the soil pH for a nominal fee. Table 1 contains specific ground limestone recommendations when the soil pH and texture are known.

When the pH of the soil is above 7.5, elemental sulfur should be used to lower the pH. Purchase a pelleted elemental sulfur product, which can be easily applied with a drop or centrifugal spreader. Apply sulfur and mix it thoroughly into the upper 4–6 inches at the rate recommended in table 2.

Fertilization

Seed sown on most soils that have not been fertilized either fails or produces a thin, weedy turf. Sod also establishes faster when properly fertilized. Have the soil tested for the level of nutrients. The results will give you a recommendation of how much and the type of fertilizer to apply. If you are not able to have a soil test taken, apply 20 pounds of 5-10-5, 5-10-10, or equivalent[2] with either a drop or a centrifugal spreader.

1. In the pH scale, a value of 7.0 indicates a neutral soil, neither acid nor alkaline. Values less than 7.0 (as pH 6.5) indicate acidity (the higher the number, the more alkaline the soil).

Final Preparation

Finish all the drainage, rough grading, topsoil additions, and final grading. You should then have a smooth, even expanse of soil without humps or hollows and with no trash or large stones.

Spread whatever organic matter, fertilizer, lime, or sulfur and mix all thoroughly into the top 4–6 inches of soil. Even distribution is important. Spread organic materials with a shovel or fork. Apply fertilizer, lime, or sulfur with a fertilizer spreader. Tilling machines with revolving metal blades are good for soil mixing. Perhaps you can rent or borrow one. Lacking this, turn the soil several times with a spading fork or tractor-drawn tool.

It may be more convenient to rake the fertilizer into the surface of the loose seedbed than to mix it deeply. This practice will not harm the seed or sod, and the turfgrass will grow as well.

Rake the seedbed again to produce a smooth surface. If you have a roller, make one trip over each part of the seedbed. This firms the seedbed and shows up small humps and hollows to be corrected. Rake the seedbed once more to ready it for planting. Do not rake the soil so much that the surface is powdery. A mixture of soil granules and small clods is better.

2. Other fertilizers serve as well. See table 4 for rates of other grades of fertilizer.

Table 2. Amount of elemental sulfur needed to lower soil pH in upper 4″–6″ of soil

Lowering pH to 6.5*	Pounds of elemental sulfur/1,000 sq ft of area	
Original pH	**Sandy**	**Clay**
7.5	10–15	20–25
8.0	25–35	35–50
8.5	35–40	40–50

*These rates cannot be used on established turfgrass. See lawn maintenance section for rates on established turfgrass.

Planting

Once the site is prepared as described, you are ready for planting. You must decide whether to seed or sod your new lawn. The choice is based on several factors such as cost, time of year, and type of turfgrass desired. Sodding is considerably more expensive than seeding. However, with proper irrigation, sodding can be done almost any time of the year when the soil is not frozen. Therefore, if you must establish your lawn during the early to midsummer period, sodding is your only option. Sod is usually only available as a blend of several improved Kentucky bluegrasses, which may not be suitable for all sites. This is especially true for areas that are droughty and will not be irrigated or fertilized too heavily. You can have a "quality sod" lawn from seed within 2 years if properly maintained.

Seeding

Proper time

Establishing a new lawn from seed is the least expensive and the most widely followed method today. However, it is most important to seed at the proper time. For upstate New York it is best to seed between August 15 and September 15. In southeastern New York, seeding should be done from August 15 to October 1.

Other times

Successful seedings can also be made during the late fall and winter months (assuming no snow), when turfgrass is in a dormant condition, and in the spring. The late fall period varies year to year, but generally begins in November after the last mowing. The seed planted during this period will not germinate until next spring. Dormant seeding of this type should not be done on areas prone to erosion, such as steep slopes. Under most conditions, it is not advisable to spring seed *unless* both irrigation and a preemergence crabgrass herbicide (see reference 9) are applied.

The two times to avoid seeding are October and during June, July, and early August. October seedings generally fail since the very young seedlings are not deeply rooted and are easily killed during the winter and early spring. Seedings made in the summer seldom survive because of a lack of water, reduced vigor of the turfgrass plant, and the competition from fast growing weeds.

Remember the *best* time to seed is late summer to early fall and spring. *Never* seed during October or during June, July, or early August.

Kinds of turfgrass for lawns

A common and most serious error in lawn establishment is choosing the wrong kind of turfgrass seed. If you have already decided to use a mixture of seeds and just want brief recommendations on how to choose a mixture, turn to page 7. However, more study about specific types of grasses and their uses is well worth the effort.

There is no perfect turfgrass for northern lawns; but of the dozens that have been tried, three are far better and more durable than the others. The three basic lawn grasses are Kentucky bluegrass, improved perennial ryegrasses, and the fine fescues (including red, creeping, chewings, and hard fescue). Rough bluegrass can be used but only in moist shade.

Kentucky bluegrass is the basic grass for sunny places in good soil and has long been considered the backbone of mixtures for sunny lawns. It responds well to good care and fertilizer and forms a dense sod. Of importance to the homeowner is its ability to spread and fill in bare spots during establishment and injury. Kentucky bluegrass generally goes dormant and turns brown during hot dry summers when irrigation is not provided, but usually recovers quickly when temperatures cool and rains return.

Several diseases severely injure common-type Kentucky bluegrass, and for this reason two or more disease-resistant varieties should be used. Select appropriate varieties from the current issue of *Home Lawns: Grass Varieties and Pest Control Guide*.

Fine fescues are the best grasses for less fertile, sandy, and droughty soils, either in sun or shade. They form a fine-textured attractive sod. The leaves are pine-needlelike and hard to cut with a dull mower. Fine fescues are somewhat less tolerant of heat than Kentucky bluegrass and may brown off more quickly during hot dry summers. Their ability to recover under such conditions is inferior to Kentucky bluegrass but adequate for all of New York. Red fescue or creeping red fescue, as it is often called, is the most commonly used fine fescue. Improved varieties are available (see reference 9) and preferred to common red fescue. One or more improved varieties of hard and chewings fescues are available and can be substituted, at least in part, for creeping red fescue. Fine fescues blend well with Kentucky bluegrass, but may dominate under low maintenance or dry shady conditions.

Improved perennial ryegrasses, sometimes called turf-type ryegrass, are relatively new, but are rapidly gaining acceptance as desirable lawn grasses. They are best adapted to the moderate levels of fertility, moisture, and sunlight conditions, as are many of the Kentucky bluegrasses. They are the fastest to establish from seed, with fine fescue second and Kentucky bluegrass the slowest. Unlike common perennial ryegrass, turf types are dark green, fine textured, and have good winter-hardiness. They require about the same care as many of the Kentucky bluegrasses. Perennial ryegrasses also require a sharp mower for a clean cut. They are best used in mixtures with Kentucky bluegrass, but can be part of a three-way mixture including fine fescue. Wear tolerance of the improved perennial ryegrass is greater than for either Kentucky bluegrass or the fine fescues. The improved varieties (see reference 9) are suitable for southeastern New York conditions. However, the perennial ryegrasses are less well adapted to upstate New York winter conditions and can be killed. This is one reason why perennial ryegrass should not make up more than 20 percent of the mixture.

Rough bluegrass or trivialis bluegrass (*Poa trivialis*) is a special-purpose turfgrass for moist shade only. It seldom lasts long in dry sunny areas; seed sown there is wasted. Even in moist shade the bright green, soft leaves never make a really tough sod.

Two unacceptable grasses are creeping bentgrass and Colonial bentgrass. Creeping bentgrass can be used to create a beautiful lawn, but requires far more care than most people can give. It is generally considered suitable for use on golf courses only. Close and frequent mowing, regular watering and fertilization, and constant protection against diseases are required for its success. In the past, some seed mixtures have contained creeping bentgrass. Lawns seeded to these mixtures now contain large patches or areas of fluffy matted turf. Even when not seeded, creeping bentgrass may enter voluntarily into any lawn and should be considered a weed. It can generally be removed by digging it out or by using a nonselective herbicide.

Colonial bentgrass has been used in small percentages as a lawn grass component. It is adapted to poorer soils than Kentucky bluegrass, but is short lived and makes no real contribution to the mixture.

Redtop, Canada bluegrass, annual ryegrass, and common perennial ryegrass are sometimes included in less-expensive lawn mixtures. Most are fast growing and result in a quick temporary flush of green. Redtop and Canada bluegrass are adapted to wetter acid soils and may be justified for rough lawn mixtures that are to receive minimum care. The common ryegrasses are suitable for use in sloping areas because of their ability to establish quickly and minimize washing or erosion. Not more than 10 percent redtop or 20 percent ryegrasses should make up any such mixture.

Timothy, orchardgrass, and meadow or tall fescue are all coarse-textured pasture or hay-type grasses. They have no place in a lawn mixture because they produce unattractive, coarse, clumpy, or stubble-like growth. They are occasionally added to lawn-grass mixtures. Read the label and do not purchase any lawn mixture containing these grasses.

White clover is used in some lawn-seed mixtures. The advantages of clover are that it provides some fertilizer nitrogen (taken from the air) for the lawn grasses, remains greener than most grasses during hot dry periods, and may survive after mismanagement and neglect have killed the good lawn grasses. Clover is coarse textured and forms patches that give the lawn a spotty appearance. It is soft and slippery, attracts bees, and is the cause of "grass stain" on clothing; it does not compete with weeds as does good turfgrass. In winter the clover patches are bare and are more likely to winter-kill than lawn grasses. Thus, some people like clover in the lawn, whereas others consider it a weed. If clover is to be used in a lawn mixture, several cultural practices must be followed to ensure its survival. First, do not use herbicides that control clover (see reference 9). Second, avoid the use of high nitrogen fertilizers since clover produces most of its own nitrogen. Third, clover grows best at a neutral pH of 7 or above. Therefore, acid soils must be limed to benefit both the clover and the turfgrass.

Seeding blends or mixtures

Although a single species, such as Kentucky bluegrass, can be used to establish a lawn, a mixture of species is preferred. Since all turfgrasses are not equally susceptible to disease, insects, and environmental hazards, a mixture has a much greater chance of success. If one species is injured or eliminated by disease or other hazards, the others may be able to fill in the voids. Species also vary in such factors as speed of establishment, recuperative potential after injury, fertility requirements, and tolerance to close mowing. The mixture chosen should have at least two of the basic species, which are Kentucky bluegrass, fine fescues, and improved turf-type perennial ryegrass. If for aesthetic or other reasons you still prefer a single species lawn and are willing to chance the risks, always include at least three recommended varieties of that species.

Choosing a ready-made seed mixture

The most important information printed on a seed package is the content label. Required by law, it lists individual species in the mixture. For each grass the percentage present is given along with germination percentages, weed seeds, and other facts. To judge the quality of a seed mixture, add the percentages of Kentucky bluegrasses, fine fescues, and improved perennial ryegrasses. If the total of these basic lawn grasses is 80% or more and does not contain the objectionable grasses listed on this page, the mixture is suitable to buy.

For most sunny lawns with a normal moisture supply, Kentucky bluegrass should make up at least 55% of the mixture. For dry soils, either in sun or shade, fine fescues should total at least 65% in the mixture.

SPECIES	SHADY SITES* (% by weight)	SUNNY SITES†
Kentucky bluegrass	10%	55%†
Fine fescue	65%	25%
Improved perennial ryegrass	15%	20%
Total lb of mixture/1000 sq ft	5–6 lb	3½–4lb

*Rough bluegrass can be substituted in moist shade.
†The remaining species of any mixture should not include bentgrass, tall fescue, and other pasture-type grasses.

If you buy a mixture of the quality suggested, it is unlikely that you will get seed that is of inferior quality so far as germination percentages, weed seed content, and inert matter are concerned.

Remember to look for at least 80% total basic lawn grasses, including at least 55% Kentucky bluegrass or 65% fine fescue, depending on your own lawn situation. If you cannot obtain this desired mixture, you may need to buy the components separately and then make your own seed mixture.

Sowing seed

Seed can be sown immediately after fertilization; no delay or waiting period is necessary. Sow seed evenly, or there will be an uneven pattern of grass and bare ground. A mechanical drop or centrifugal type spreader does the best job of seeding (or fertilizing or liming), but hand seeding is satisfactory if it is done carefully. To seed by hand, first divide your seed into two equal parts. If this is your first attempt to sow seed, mix each half of the seed with some sand or fine topsoil to give you more material with which to work. When there is no wind, scatter one half evenly and carefully while walking back and forth in parallel lines. Scatter the other half in the same manner while walking in lines at right angles to the first (fig. 1).

After the seed is sown, rake the soil lightly. Use just the tips of the rake teeth and cover the seed about 1/8 inch deep. Seed covered too deeply will be lost; so omit this raking unless you can do it carefully. Go over the area lightly with a roller to firm the soil about the seeds. If you cannot roll the seeding, no harm will be done; the seed will merely germinate more slowly.

Mulching

A straw mulch is not necessary for most new seedings, but is helpful for warm-weather seedings, on sandy soils, or on steep slopes. Shake out the straw thoroughly, spreading it uniformly to a depth of about 1 inch. When you have finished, you should still be able to see about half the soil surface through the straw. The mulch slows up surface drying and breaks the force of rains and watering. On steep slopes, anchor the straw in place with wooden stakes and heavy twine. Tack the twine to stakes driven flush into the ground on 3-foot centers. Hay is not a satisfactory substitute for straw because it will very likely contain an abundance of seeds of hay-type grasses and weeds.

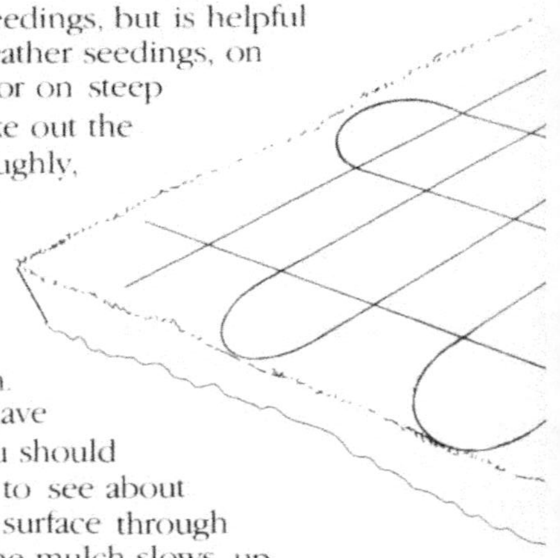

Sodding

A poor weedy lawn can be removed with a sod cutter and replaced with dense, green, weed-free sod in one day. Although such a practice is possible, and even feasible in certain situations, sodding generally requires the same preliminary procedures as for seeding. A sodded lawn can be installed anytime during the growing season. The extra cost of the sod and the labor of installation provide turf quality that would take at least a full year to develop from seed.

Sodding may be the only answer for steep slopes or spots where traffic ruins young seedlings.

Nursery-grown sod with blends of improved Kentucky bluegrass is available in most suburban areas. This makes an attractive lawn in sunny situations, but a fine fescue mixture is a better choice for dry or shaded areas.

Large areas are best sodded by landscape contractors because the labor and machinery requirements are more than the average person can supply. Small areas and patches can be sodded by an energetic amateur.

To install sod, prepare the soil just as though seed were to be planted. The soil should be moderately moist when the sod is laid. After all is ready, purchase the sod. Large lots of sod can be obtained for direct delivery to the job. Small lots of sod for patching are available from garden supply firms. Do not accept sod that is dried or wilted. For best results the sod should be laid soon, no more than 36 hours, after it is cut.

Nursery grown sod is about 1-inch thick with little or no soil attached and of uniform width. Before laying the sod, lightly water the soil. This improves the ability of the sod to survive and knit in faster. Lay the sod strips on a prepared soil, tightly together, edge to edge, and with staggered joints like bricks in a wall. Fill all cracks with screened soil. Soak the newly laid sod thoroughly. As soon as it is dry enough to walk on, lightly roll or tamp the sod to give a good contact with the soil beneath. Water often enough (every 2 or 3 days) in the early part of the day to keep the soil moist until the sod is securely rooted, usually within 2 weeks. Avoid overwatering.

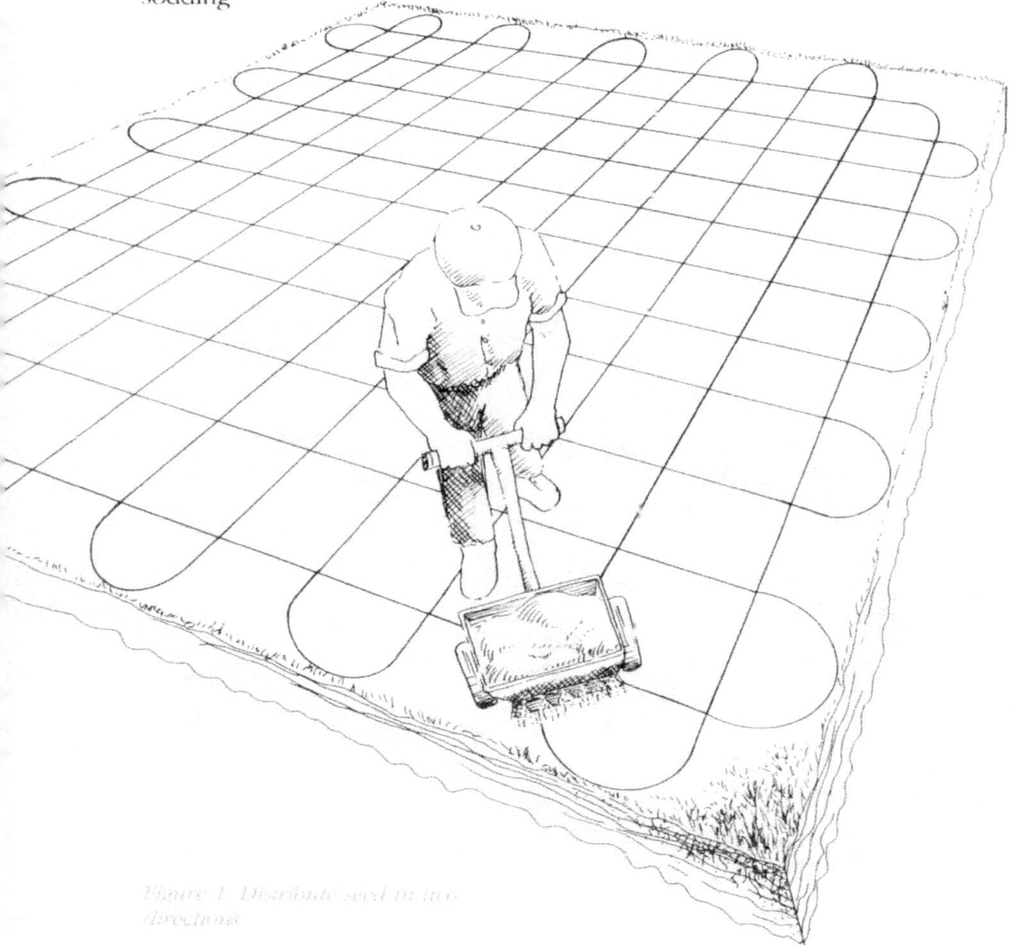

Figure 1. Distribute seed in two directions

Postplanting Care

Watering Your New Lawn

Seed must be wet before it will germinate and grow. Dry seed in dry soil will not germinate until conditions are favorable. Birds may feed on the seed, but the amount of seed they eat is seldom important. Rain usually falls often enough for good growth, but results are quicker and more certain with artificial watering. The first sprinkling must be thorough but gentle; avoid washing the seed or soil away. Keep the seedbed moist until the grass is well started, or the entire planting may be lost. Watering may be as frequent as once or twice daily, especially for the first several weeks. Water more deeply once the grass comes up. Keep the soil moist but not soaking wet.

If there is little or no ryegrass in your seed mixture, seedlings may not appear for 10 days or more after the soil is thoroughly wet. *Do not* be alarmed. A poorer mixture will produce a quicker cover, but this is mostly show. After the second or third mowing, little or no watering should be required unless there is a week or more without rain. On sodded lawns, daily watering may be required to keep the sod moist until the sod has securely rooted. This generally occurs within 2 to 3 weeks.

Removing Mulch and Twine

If properly applied the mulching material seldom needs to be removed. Remove mulch only when the young turfgrass plants are being smothered. Twine used for securing mulch to the ground should be taken up before the first mowing to avoid jamming the mower.

First Mowing

For the first mowing, set the mower to cut at least 2 inches high. Mow as soon as the turfgrass is tall enough to reach the mower blades. Be sure the mower is sharp and the grass is dry. If the soil is too moist, seedlings will be pulled up. Mow often enough so as not to leave matted clippings to smother the new turfgrass. Keep matted clippings and fallen leaves off the new seeding by careful sweeping with a rake.

Fertilizing

To help ensure a dense weed-free stand of turfgrass, fertilize 3 to 4 weeks after the seeds have germinated or following sodding. Use a complete fertilizer with a ratio of 2-1-1 or 4-1-3 at the rate of 1 pound of nitrogen per 1,000 square feet (see table 4 for the correct amount of fertilizer). Lightly water in the fertilizer after application to avoid possible fertilizer burn of the turfgrass plants.

Every lawn, good or bad, needs to be mowed regularly and fertilized occasionally. In many areas, liming is equally important. Watering may or may not be desirable on your particular lawn. These four operations, with particular emphasis on fertilization and mowing, are all that need concern you except for special circumstances.

Mowing

Close mowing ruins many lawns. The rule should be mow high and often. Set your mower to cut at least 1 1/2 inches high for spring and fall and slightly higher for summer or leave at 1 1/2 inches throughout the year. Your lawn will look neat at this height, and you will still be leaving enough top growth to produce food for a deep root system and a solid dense turf. Mow throughout the season whenever there is 1/2 inch or more of growth to be cut. Keep on mowing as long as the grass continues to grow in the fall. Mow often enough for the clippings to disappear by the next day. Always leave the clippings where they fall, for they return nutrients to the soil. You can reduce your fertilizer needs by 25 percent if clippings are returned to the lawn. This saves you both money and the time needed to remove clippings. If, by chance, you delay mowing so long that bunches of clippings remain the day after cutting, rake up these clippings or spread them so that they will not smother the grass.

Choosing a Mower

Two types of lawn mowers are widely available. The older reel-type mower has revolving knives that cut the grass blades against a stationary bed knife in a scissors-type action. This mower shears the grass blades cleanly when it is properly adjusted and leaves no brown or ragged tips. A reel-type mower is best adapted to smooth areas that are mowed regularly.

Rotary mowers depend upon the high-speed whipping action of a sharpened blade whirling in the air. They handle taller grass on irregular areas and are useful on areas not mowed regularly. Unless the blade is very sharp, a rotary mower tears the leaf tips; the lawn as a result appears scorched or singed gray the day after mowing.

The rotary mower can be a dangerous tool. Many operators have been injured by the whirling blades and bystanders by thrown stones or other debris. Only an adult should operate a rotary mower. Do not remove any of the mower's guards that have been installed for safety reasons. Some of the safety features may seem unimportant, but remember they were included to make the mower safer.

In the past several years a new type of rotary mower has appeared on the market, namely the mulching mower. This mower was developed to cut the turfgrass clippings finer than the conventional rotary mower does. This enables most of the clippings to work their way into the turfgrass canopy. Thus, mulching mowers can further eliminate the need for removing clippings since they cannot be seen after mowing. If you have or are considering the use of a mulching mower, review these helpful tips:

- The grass must be relatively dry before mowing to help prevent machine clogging and the formation of large clumps of clippings.
- You need to mow more often in spring and fall because of the faster grass-growth rate. Again this can help prevent the mower from clogging and the clippings from clumping. You may need to switch to conventional mowers during these periods.

Just because a power mower is easy to run, do not use it when it is dull or out of adjustment. Do not ruin your light machine in work too heavy for it.

Figure 2. Types of mower

Rotary mower

Reel-type mower

Adjusting the Mower Cutting Height

Both reel-type and rotary mowers can be adjusted for height of cut. This important adjustment is easy to make. The height of cut of most rotary mowers is set by adjusting the height of the wheels. Height adjustment is slightly complicated for reel-type mowers. In either case, follow the instruction manual for proper adjustment.

Fertilizing

Adequate turfgrass nutrition is crucial to the establishment and development of a healthy vigorous lawn. Such a lawn is less likely to be invaded by weeds or troubled by most insect and disease pests. Because the soil generally cannot supply all the needed nutrients, routine applications of a complete fertilizer are necessary.

A complete fertilizer contains nitrogen, phosphorus, and potassium.

Figure 3. Types of mowers

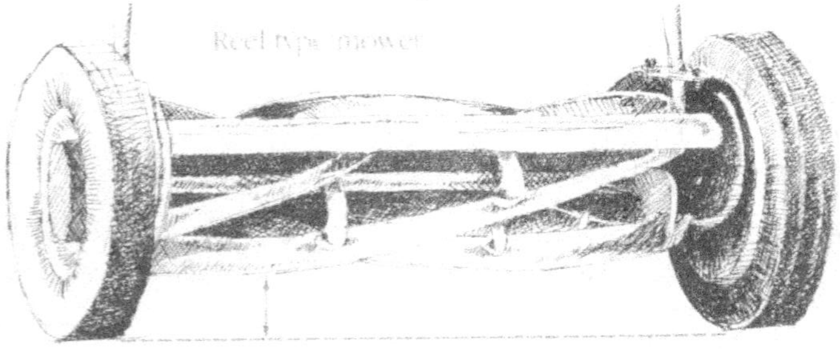

These nutrients are required in larger amounts by turfgrass than are other minor nutrients usually found in adequate supply in the soil. Nitrogen is required in the largest amount. It is responsible for overall growth and color, and the effect of its application is most readily seen. Phosphorus is critical at the time of lawn establishment to encourage root growth and development. Potassium is associated with the overall growth of the turf and is required in the second largest amount. Tolerance to extremes in temperature, moisture, and wear is enhanced by sufficient amounts of potassium.

The law requires that every package of fertilizer be labeled to show the guaranteed minimum percentages (or grade) of the three important fertilizer nutrients. For example, a fertilizer with the analysis of 10-6-4 contains at least 10% total nitrogen, 6% phosphoric acid, and 4% potash. Many grades of complete fertilizers are available. You can also purchase fertilizers containing one or two nutrients. For example, superphosphate 0-20-0 contains only phosphorus, and potassium nitrate 13-0-44 contains both nitrogen and potassium.

Properties of Fertilizers

Nitrogen is the plant nutrient required in the largest amount by turfgrass. The nitrogen found in a bag of fertilizer in many cases is a mixture of several types, that is, water soluble and water insoluble (slow release).

Nitrogen sources can be classified into two groups with the following properties:

Water soluble sources—

- are very readily available to the turfgrass plant, response after application being rapid;
- are subject to leaching;
- can burn turf if applied at high rates and not watered in;
- are less expensive;
- should be applied at lower rates more often;
- have the potential for lowering soil pH;
- have a good cool weather response.

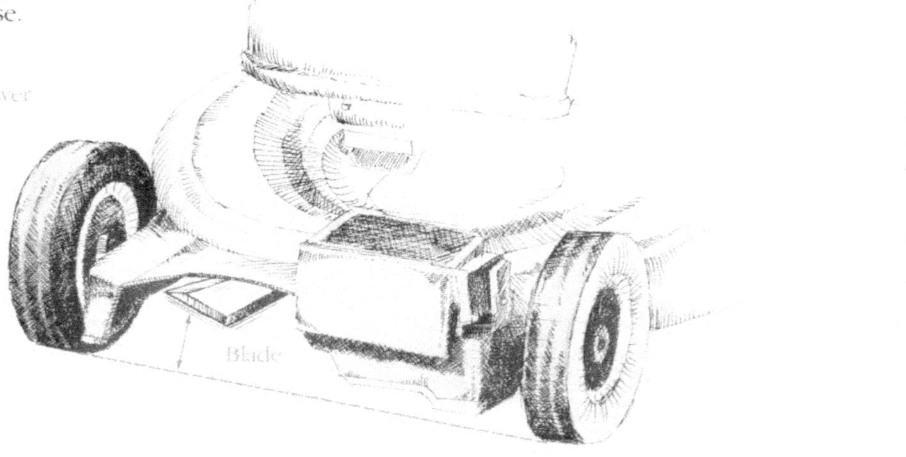

Slow release sources—

- are more slowly available to the turfgrass plant (release is dependent on temperature and moisture);
- provide a more constant supply of nitrogen;
- have less potential for leaching;
- have less potential for burning;
- are generally more expensive;
- can be applied at slightly higher rates less often;
- have a moderate to poor cool-weather response.

Examples of several types of fertilizer, their analysis, and properties are outlined in table 3.

There are different types of phosphorus and potassium, but their properties are similar, and the consumer is not faced with the choice of purchasing different types.

Table 3. Properties of fertilizers used on turfgrass

Nitrogen carrier	Type	Nutrient content (%) N	P_2O_5	K_2O	Soil acidifying effect	Water solubility	Potential for burn
Ammonium nitrate	Syn. inorganic	33	0	0	Moderate	High	Very high
Ammonium sulfate	Syn. inorganic	21	0	0	Great	High	High
Urea	Syn. organic	45	0	0	Moderate	High	High
Monoammonium phosphate	Syn. inorganic	11	48	0	Slight	Moderate	Low
Diammonium phosphate	Syn. inorganic	20	50	0	Moderate	Moderate	Moderate
IBDU (isobutylidine diurea)	Syn. organic	31	0	0	Undetermined	Very low	Low
Sulfur-coated urea(SCU)	Syn. organic	32	0	0	Undetermined	Very low	Low
Ureaformaldehyde	Syn. organic	38	0	0	Undetermined	Very low	Low
Milorganite	Nat. organic	6	4	0	Undetermined	Very low	Low
Methylene urea	Syn. organic	38	0	0	Undetermined	Very low	Low
Superphosphate	Inorganic	0	20	0	Low	Low	Low
Treble superphosphate	Inorganic	0	45	0	Low	Low	Low
Muriate of potash (KCl)	Inorganic	0	0	60	Low	Moderate	Moderate
Sulfate of potash (K_2SO_4)	Inorganic	0	0	50	Low	Moderate	Low
Potassium nitrate	Inorganic	13	0	44	None	Moderate	Very high

Table 4. Maximum amount of fertilizer to use for each application

If the first figure (% nitrogen) of the analysis is:	For 1,000 square feet of area: of established lawn (to apply 1 lb nitrogen)	of new seedbed or lawn to be renovated (to apply 2 lb nitrogen)
	pounds	*pounds*
4	25	50
5	20	40
6	17	33
7	14	28
8	12½	25
9	11	22
10	10	20
20	5	10
25	4	8

Fertilizing Established Turf

Test your soil

Soil testing is the only way to determine how much phosphorus, potassium, and lime or sulfur your lawn may need for optimum growth. The soil in your lawn should be tested every 2 to 3 years. Be sure to sample the soil well in advance of when you plan to apply fertilizer. If a fall application is planned, submit a sample in early summer. Remember not to take a soil sample 3 to 4 weeks after fertilizer or lime has been applied. See the soil sampling section in the Appendix for specific instructions. The soil test will help you select a fertilizer best suited for your individual soil condition.

Frequency

Frequency of fertilization depends upon your circumstances and aesthetic standards. The amount of a nitrogen fertilizer that most lawns require depends upon many factors such as the predominant species of turfgrass, soil type, desired turfgrass quality, and climatic factors. Most New York lawns need between 2 to 5 pounds of actual nitrogen per 1,000 square feet during the growing season. On Long Island where the ground water is becoming increasingly contaminated with nitrates, only 1 to 3 pounds of nitrogen should be used. This is especially true on sandy soils that are highly irrigated.

Lawns that contain mostly fine fescues should need only 1 to 2 pounds of nitrogen per 1,000 square feet during the year. Kentucky bluegrass lawns that are frequently irrigated may need up to 5 pounds of nitrogen. In general, lawns on sandy soils that are routinely irrigated and (or) receive heavy traffic require more nitrogen and potassium.

Rate

Lawn fertilizer manufacturers have made the application of fertilizers more convenient and easier by providing information directly on the fertilizer bag. The bag lists the total amount of fertilizer, the fertilizer analysis, the area to be covered at a given rate, and the setting for various fertilizer spreaders. When this information is not available, you need to determine the proper rate for a single application. Consider only the first figure in the fertilizer analysis. In a 10-6-4, the 10 represents the nitrogen content percentage. Do not apply more than 1 pound of nitrogen per 1,000 square feet per single application. On Long Island, reduce this rate to 1/2 pound of nitrogen per 1,000 square feet, except when all the nitrogen is in a slow-release form. To determine the amount of fertilizer needed, see table 4. Use the first figure of the fertilizer analysis. If you had a 10-6-4 fertilizer and planned to apply 1 pound of nitrogen, you would use 10 pounds per 1,000 square feet.

Timing

The best time to fertilize lawns is when the turfgrass needs the nutrients most. For established lawns in the Northeast this generally occurs in spring and again in the late summer to early fall. Temperatures during these periods usually run from 70°-80° F during the day to 40°-65° F during the night; such temperatures have been found to be most conducive for turfgrass growth. Other factors should be considered when determining how much and how often to apply fertilizers: the total amount of fertilizer to be applied annually, type of fertilizer, soil type, and irrigation practices. Generally more fertilizer is needed when water-soluble fertilizers are used on sandy soils that are highly irrigated.

The number of fertilizer applications needed is based in part on the total pounds of nitrogen to be applied annually. The maximum rate of application of nitrogen is 1 pound per 1,000 square feet per single application. Therefore, if you plan to apply 3 pounds of nitrogen per 1,000 square feet per year, a minimum of three applications must be made.

If you plan to fertilize your lawn only once per year, then a later summer or early fall treatment is best. For more than one fertilizer application per year, refer to table 5 for suggested times of application.

Since seasonal weather conditions vary from year to year, use the following guide for interpreting the seasons described in table 5:

EARLY SPRING
-the period when the lawn has just started to green up and grow, but before the big "spring flush" of growth

LATE SPRING
-the period just after the "spring flush," but while temperatures are still very mild (i.e., 60°-70° F day, 40°-60° F night)

EARLY SUMMER
-usually occurs late May to early June when day temperatures are consistently in mid-70s to lower 80s.

LATE SUMMER OR EARLY FALL
-after summer heat spell, usually in late August or early September when temperatures start to moderate and nights are cool.

DORMANT OR LATE FALL
-the period just after last mowing until winter snow cover.

There are several times during the year when fertilizing should be avoided. In most cases a heavy early to mid-spring application of a fertilizer (especially nitrogen) can lead to certain disease problems and make your turfgrass shallow rooted. Both results can lead to serious trouble for your lawn during the summer. If an early spring application is desirable, apply about one half the recommended rate of fertilizer. Do not fertilize heavily during the summer; then at least part or all of

Table 5. Suggested timing of fertilizer application based on the number of yearly applications

Number of yearly applications	Early spring	Late spring	Early summer	Late summer or early fall	Late fall or dormant*
1				I	
2	II		II	I	II
3	II	II	III	I	II
4		III	IV	I	II
5	III	IV	V	I	II

NOTE: When there are two or more of the same numeral on a line, apply at only one of the times.
*Avoid late fall (dormant) fertilizer application on Long Island if water soluble fertilizers are used.

For example, if you are applying 3 lb of nitrogen per year, you have three choices for times of application:

1. (late summer or early fall) + (late fall or dormant) + (early summer)

OR

2. (late summer or early fall) + (early spring) + (early summer)

OR

3. (late summer or early fall) + (late spring) + (early summer).

the fertilizer should be a slow-release form. Be sure to use half the recommended rate at this time. Another time not to overfertilize is midfall. Then heavy fertilization can lead to winter disease problems and a greater chance of damage.

How to Apply

It is very important to apply fertilizers evenly. Careless distribution causes uneven growth and color. Heavy concentrations of fertilizer result in burned spots in the turf. A mechanical spreader is best for this work. You can apply a natural organic fertilizer at almost any season without danger of burning your grass. Inorganic fertilizers can be used during the growing season, but take these precautions against burning: be especially careful about even distribution, spread fertilizer only when the grass is completely dry, and immediately wash the fertilizer off the grass blades to the ground.

Dry fertilizers can be applied with either a gravity drop-type spreader or a centrifugal spreader. Use a drop-type spreader when applying fertilizer-herbicide products (i.e., a feed and weed product) to minimize the chance of herbicide injury to trees, shrubs, and vegetable gardens. Also, a drop-type spreader is good for applying ground limestone.

Centrifugal spreaders generally cover a larger area with each pass and cut down the time it takes to fertilize your lawn. Fertilizer particles are more susceptible to wind blowing by this method, a uniform application being made more difficult. Centrifugal spreaders can be used to apply granular lime and sulfur materials as well.

When using either spreader, make at least two passes over your lawn. Apply half the amount of fertilizer in one direction and make the second application at a right angle to the first pass. This will help eliminate the streaks that develop from an uneven fertilizer application. See figure 1.

Figure 1. Types of fertilizer spreaders

Rotary — Drop type

Lime or Sulfur

Soil pH modification

For the best turfgrass growth the soil should be kept at a pH of 6.0–7.0. In some regions of New York, soils naturally have an acceptable pH and may never need lime or sulfur. In other regions the pH may be higher than 7.5 (too alkaline) or lower than 6.0 (too acid). The only way to be sure of the soil's pH is to have it tested. Your local county Cooperative Extension agent can assist you with this pH test.

To raise the soil pH

When you know the soil pH, refer to table 1. On established lawns, apply half the recommended rate.

Liming can be done in either spring or fall. Do not apply lime during the summer or within 2 weeks after applying fertilizer. Hydrated lime should not be used because it is caustic and difficult to handle. See table 6 for a description of several liming materials and suggested rates of application.

When a large amount of lime is to be applied to established turfgrass, that is, more than 50 pounds per 1,000 square feet, a split application is recommended. Apply half the rate in the spring and the other half in the fall. Apply water to remove lime from the shoots and to move it into the soil.

To lower the soil pH

When the pH is greater than 7.5, acidifying materials must be applied. Elemental sulfur is the preferred material to lower soil pH. For ease of application, use a pelleted form of sulfur, which can be applied with a centrifugal spreader. Do not apply more than 5 pounds of elemental sulfur per 1,000 square feet per application to established lawns. Be sure to water in sulfur to avoid burning. Only apply sulfur during spring and fall. Table 2 lists the rate of sulfur to be used when sulfur is to be incorporated into the soil during lawn establishment.

Avoid the use of ferrous sulfate and aluminum sulfate for soil acidification. Remember that the use of certain fertilizers, for example, ammonium sulfate and urea, can lower the pH over a period of time.

Watering

Most lawns, if not irrigated, turn brown in midsummer, but recover quickly when cool damp weather arrives. If your lawn does not survive an ordinary drought without watering, it probably needs renovating. You can avoid numerous problems and save time and effort if you can learn to accept an occasional brown turf in dry summers.

You can improve the appearance of your lawn by proper watering, but you can also ruin it if you are careless. A few waterings should keep your lawn fairly green during the summer. Water when the soil begins to dry out but before the grass wilts and turns brown. To test if your lawn needs watering, dig into the soil to a depth of 3 to 4 inches. If the soil is dry, soak it to a depth of 5 to 6 inches, which equals about 1 to 2 inches in a can or rain gauge. If the grass has a purplish cast and if footprints remain after you walk across the lawn, then the turfgrass is wilting and in need of water. It is best to water in midmorning, if possible; but excellent results can be achieved at other times of the day.

Avoid frequent light sprinklings because they benefit shallow-rooted annual grasses and weeds, while the deeper-rooted turfgrasses suffer from inadequate moisture. Eventually desirable deep-rooted turfgrasses will be taken over by undesirable shallow-rooted annual grasses and weeds.

Table 6. Liming materials and their characteristics

Material	Composition	Rate of reaction	Method of application	Comments
Ground limestone	Granular ground limestone	Slow and gradual	Drop spreader	Water in if lawn appearance is a concern; only a slight chance of leaf burn. Its effect can last up to 2 years.
Pelleted limestone	Pelleted finely ground limestone	Very fast	Centrifugal spreader	Apply 60–70% the ground limestone rate; effect is not long lasting. Yearly applications are necessary.
Slurry limestone	Finely ground limestone in 20–30% water	Very fast	Power sprayer with high power agitation, i.e., pesticide-type sprayer	Apply 60–70% the ground limestone rate; effect is not long lasting. Yearly applications may be necessary

Generally, your lawn requires only 1 to 2 inches of rainfall or irrigation per week during June, July, and August. Water only once or twice per week for a long enough period to apply 1 inch of water. To test how long to leave the sprinklers running, put out several small cans, cups, or rain gauges and calculate how long it takes to obtain 1 inch of water in them. Never apply water faster than the soil can absorb it. Clay soils generally absorb water very slowly, whereas sandy soils absorb water more rapidly.

Rolling

As a regular maintenance practice, use a roller at most only once a year. If convenient, roll your lawn in early spring with a roller just heavy enough to press the frost-heaved plants back into the soil. Do this before growth starts, when the soil is dry enough to crumble easily in your fingers. Then put the roller away for the season. More rolling will do no good, and on a heavy clay soil it may be harmful. Spring rolling is the least important chore and can be omitted without serious harmful effects.

Topdressing

Golf course managers routinely topdress or spread thin layers of soil or sand over their putting greens. However, this practice is seldom done on home lawns. Topdressing helps smooth out uneven spots in your lawn and helps reduce a thatch problem. Topdressing can be done with screened, weed-free topsoil, compost, or soil from the vegetable garden. Broadcast this weed-free soil over the lawn in either early fall or early spring. Push the topdressing from the high spots to the low spots with the back of a rake, or fasten a rope to a metal door mat and drag it back and forth. Fill deep holes by lifting the sod and filling under it, or fill the deep holes with soil and sprinkle a little seed on the soil. Water the lawn to settle the loose soil and proceed with your regular maintenance program. Do not spread pure peat or humus on your lawn. These materials can do little or no good and may cause future problems.

Thatch

There are many misconceptions about thatch, its causes and problems. First, thatch is the accumulation of dead and dying turfgrass plant parts, such as roots and stems. This layer develops above the soil surface and, in many cases, contains turfgrass shoots. Thatch is not the accumulation of clippings as some believe. A layer of thatch less than 1/2 inch thick does little, if any, harm. However, when this layer is in excess of 3/4 inch, the turf is more susceptible to disease and insect problems and has less wear, drought, heat, and cold tolerance. Also, thatchy turf can be difficult to water since thatch can become water repellent when dry. Factors that lead to a thatch buildup are acid soils with a pH less than 6.0, too little or excessive fertilization, poor drainage, compacted soils, droughty conditions, and overwatering.

When excessive thatch develops, several steps should be followed to eliminate the problem. Be sure you have a thatch buildup in the first place. Take several wedge-shaped slices of your lawn, including the surface soil layer, at several locations. Inspect the samples to determine the thickness of the thatch. A layer less than 1/4 inch is considered acceptable. When the layer is between 1/4 and 1/2 inch thick, you may want to slow down further buildup by eliminating the cause(s) of the thatch. A 1/2-inch or thicker layer of thatch requires a slow but careful process of removal.

The only effective method of thatch removal is mechanical dethatching. The repeated use of a dethatching machine can, with time, reduce the thatch layer. Even though it may seem that you have removed a lot of thatch during the

Figure 5. Thatch, mat, and soil layers.

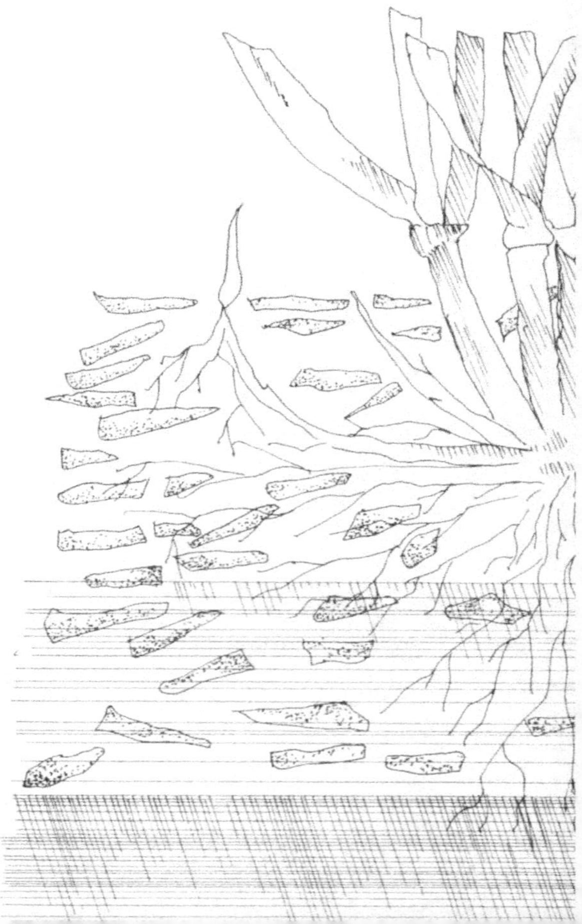

dethatching operation, it generally takes several dethatchings to significantly decrease the thatch layer.

The best time to dethatch a lawn is during the spring and early fall when weather favors a fast recovery of the injured turf. Avoid dethatching during the summer.

Biological and other chemical dethatching methods have proved to be ineffective and are not recommended. You may want to try such products on a small scale to see if they are effective on your lawn.

Topdressing is beneficial in reducing thatch. Topdressing as a means of decreasing thatch accumulation may be impractical on large lawn areas; however, you can achieve similar results in the following way: core cultivate your lawn (a core cultivator is sometimes called an aerifier or plugger and can be obtained from some garden centers or equipment rental shops), and lightly break up and work the soil back into the lawn with a metal drag mat or metal rake. In this case soil is added to the turf surface in a similar manner as described for topdressing.

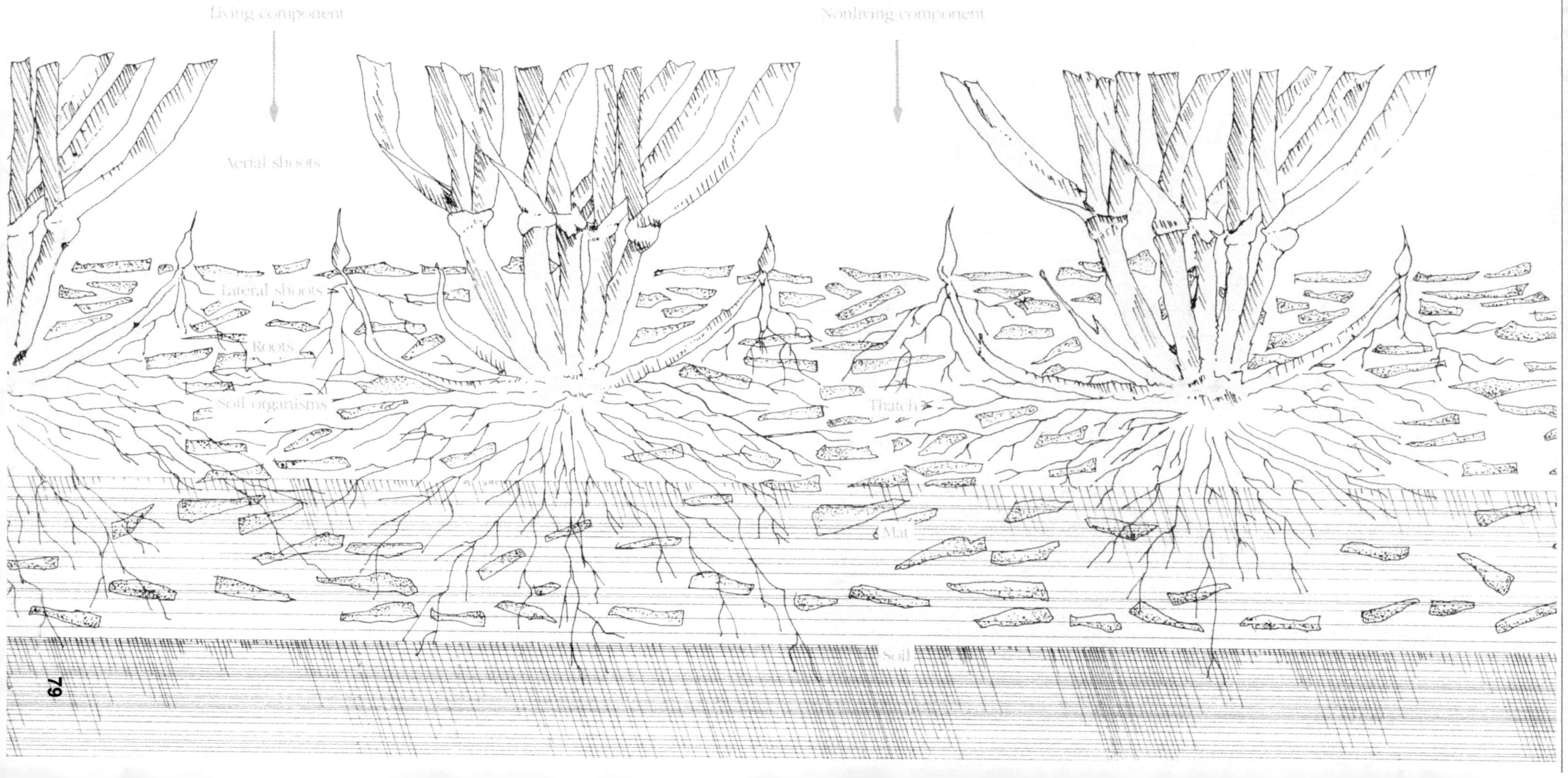

TURFGRASS MANAGEMENT CALENDAR

UPSTATE NEW YORK

	JAN.	FEB.	MARCH	APRIL	MAY	JUNE	JULY	AUG.	SEPT.	OCT.	NOV.	DEC.
Establishment												
Seeding											*	
Sodding						if water available						
Maintenance												
Mowing						as needed						
Watering												
Fertilizing												
Liming/sulfur												
Dethatching												
Renovating												
Pest Control												
Disease occurrence	Snow molds			Leaf spots Stripe smut	Melting out	Red thread	Pythium blight Dollar spot Fusarium blight		Rust Brown patch	Leaf spot Stripe smut	Snow molds	
Insect occurrence					Grubs	Chinch bug	Sod webworms		Grubs			
Weed control — Broadleaf			Postemergence					Postemergence				
Weed control — Crabgrass			Preemergence			Postemergence						

Possible

Preferred

*This time period is for dormant seeding.

LAWN MAINTENANCE RECORD CHART

Operation	JAN.	FEB.	MARCH	APRIL	MAY	JUNE	JULY	AUG.	SEPT.	OCT.	NOV.	DEC.
Fertilization												
Lime/sulfur												
Mowing												
Watering												
Weed control												
Insect control												
Disease control												
Dethatch												

Specific Note

Fertilizer	Analysis _____ Amount _____ Date _____	Analysis _____ Amount _____ Date _____	Analysis _____ Amount _____ Date _____	Analysis _____ Amount _____ Date _____
Lime/sulfur	Material _____ Amount _____ Date _____	Material _____ Amount _____ Date _____	Material _____ Amount _____ Date _____	Material _____ Amount _____ Date _____
Insect control	Material _____ Amount _____ Date _____	Material _____ Amount _____ Date _____	Material _____ Amount _____ Date _____	Material _____ Amount _____ Date _____
Weed control	Material _____ Amount _____ Date _____	Material _____ Amount _____ Date _____	Material _____ Amount _____ Date _____	Material _____ Amount _____ Date _____
Disease control	Material _____ Amount _____ Date _____	Material _____ Amount _____ Date _____	Material _____ Amount _____ Date _____	Material _____ Amount _____ Date _____

Lawn Maintenance Calendar

The following charts can be used as a guide to annual lawn maintenance practices. Some lawn maintenance operations can be conducted many different times during the year, but in some cases there is a preferred time of implementation.

Climatic factors will greatly influence the occurrence of lawn diseases, insects, and weeds and the growth of the lawn. Therefore, it is impossible to predict the exact length and kind of growing season that will happen in a given year. However, the maintenance calendar can serve as a useful guide.

The Lawn Maintenance Record Chart is included to help you keep track of your lawn maintenance practices. Post the Lawn Maintenance Calendar and the Lawn Maintenance Record Chart in a convenient place.

SOUTHEASTERN NEW YORK

		JAN.	FEB.	MARCH	APRIL	MAY	JUNE	JULY	AUG.	SEPT.	OCT.	NOV.	DEC.
Establishment													
Seeding												*	
Sodding							if water	available					
Maintenance													
Mowing													
Watering													
Fertilizing												*	*
Liming/sulfur													
Dethatching													
Renovating													
Pest Control													
Disease occurrence					Leaf	spots				Rust	Leaf	spots	
						Melting	out	Pythium	blight	Brown	patch		
								Dollar	spot				
					Stripe	smut		Fusarium	blight		Stripe	smut	
		Snow	molds				Red	thread				Snow	molds
Insect occurrence					Grubs					Grubs			
							Sod	webworms	Cutworms				
							Chinch	bug					
							Bluegrass	billbug					
Weed control	Broadleaf				Postemergence					Postemergence			
	Crabgrass				Preemergence			Postemergence					

Possible

Preferred

*Mid-Nov. through Dec. is the period for dormant seeding.

**Mid-Nov. through Dec. is the period for dormant fertilizing.

Weeds

In your lawn, there is a constant battle between the grasses you want and the weeds you do not want. Lawns get weedy if conditions are more favorable for the weeds than for the grasses. Turfgrass predominates if growing conditions are better for the grass than for the weeds. By altering growing conditions, you can control the kinds of plants in a lawn. When you start a new lawn, try to prevent weeds from getting a foothold. If you remove weeds from an established lawn, stimulate the grass to better growth, or weeds will fill in the bare spaces again. Any sound weed control program is based upon these principles.

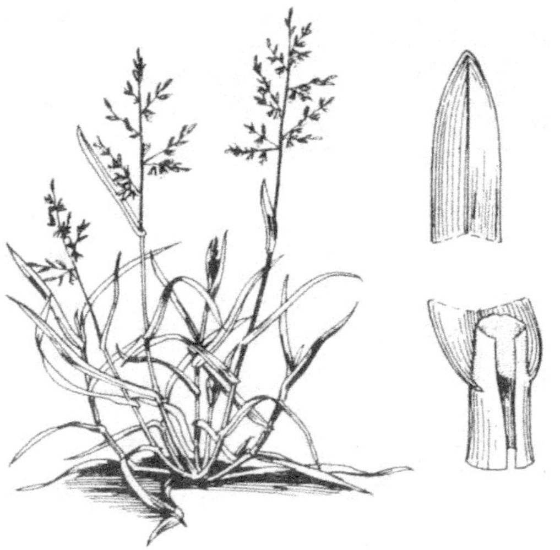

Annual bluegrass

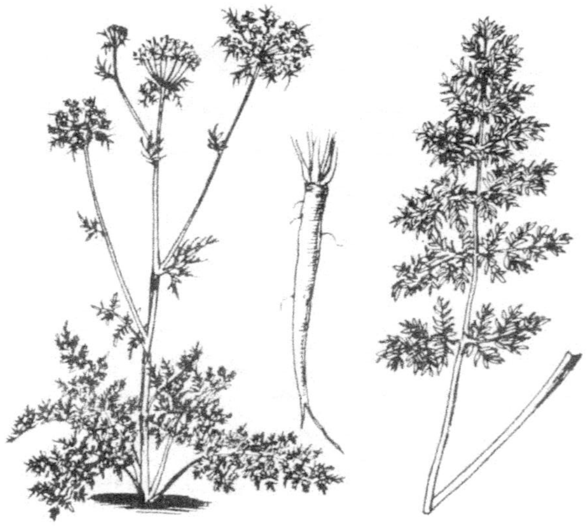

Wild carrot

Identifying Features of Weeds

Weeds differ greatly in their appearance, growth patterns, and reaction to herbicides. Grassy weeds have long narrow leaves with parallel veins and may complete their life cycle in one season. Some annual grassy weeds like crabgrass, goosegrass, and annual bluegrass recur from seed every year. Tall fescue, bentgrass, and quackgrass are grassy weeds that grow vegetatively for many years. Dicots, or nongrassy weeds, have wider net-veined leaves and are called broad-leaved weeds. Common annual broad-leaved weeds are prostrate spurge and common chickweed. Perennial broad-leaved weeds include dandelion, plantain, white clover, hawkweed, and ground ivy. Yellow nutsedge and wild onion are narrow leaved, but are not grasses. Consult Cornell Information Bulletin 131, *Weeds in Ornamental Plantings*, or your Cooperative Extension agent for help in identifying weeds.

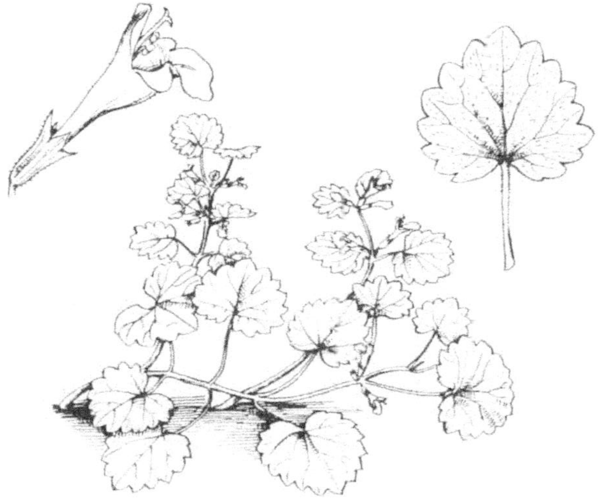

Ground ivy

Common chickweed

Common dandelion

Prostrate knotweed

Preventing Weeds in New Lawns

The greatest source of weed seeds in a new lawn is the soil itself. Almost any soil contains many more weed seeds than are carried in the grass seed. Scraping off the surface of the soil only exposes another layer of weed-infested ground and solves nothing. Where crabgrass is not a particular problem, as in upstate areas, good soil preparation gives your new lawn a satisfactory head start on the weeds.

Planting at the proper season with the right grasses and adequate fertilization at seeding time are the most important practices in minimizing weed problems. In southeastern New York and on Long Island, fall planting is almost the only means of preventing crabgrass from taking over the lawn. If you plant in early fall, the grass plants will spread laterally, and the turf will be dense and mature before most troublesome lawn weeds start growth the following spring. Use recommended fertilizer rates to speed the development of the grasses.

Do not try to prevent weed establishment by sowing an extra large amount of grass seed. A dense growth results, but the individual grass plants will be crowded and weak. Then diseases may kill large patches of grass, the lawn being left wide open to weed invasion. To save money and get better results, sow no more seed than is recommended and fertilize it well at seeding time so that each grass plant becomes established quickly.

Spring-seeded lawns have a better chance of development free of crabgrass if the recommended preemergence herbicide is used. Even though crabgrass can be controlled in a spring seeding, fall is the preferred planting time.

Weed Control in Established Lawns

If your lawn is weedy, it is likely that you established or maintained it in such a way that the weeds were favored at the expense of the grass. A few kinds of weeds may resist efforts to control them, but most of the common lawn weeds can be greatly reduced by improved lawn care. If your lawn has reasonably good drainage, you can probably produce a striking improvement in the weed situation merely by fertilizing and mowing properly. The more troublesome the weeds, the more important it is that proper maintenance practices be followed.

Sometimes weeds persist in spite of good maintenance. Then you have to decide to control them by hand pulling or using herbicides. For small lawn areas or where there are only a few weeds, hand pulling as weeds appear can be good exercise and give good temporary results. Weeds are pulled much more easily right after a heavy rain or watering. Herbicides are chemicals used to control weeds. The use of herbicides to control weeds is more practical for large areas, more difficult to pull weeds, and small patches of persistent weeds. Large areas can be treated with sprays or granules that give good weed control with minimal injury to turfgrass. Single clumps can be spot-treated with a small aerosol container, which sprays only a little herbicide over a limited area. In some situations you can brush an herbicide on a limited area. A commercially available wax bar impregnated with an herbicide can be brushed on undesirable foliage.

The best control method for general weed control on an area of any size is an overall treatment with a selective chemical that will kill the weeds and leave the grass unharmed. The broad-leaved weeds such as dandelion and chickweed require different methods of control than do annual grasses such as crabgrass and goosegrass or perennial grasses such as tall fescue and quackgrass. If the weed situation is serious and the turf is poor, you may well consider renovating the lawn.

Chemical Methods for Controlling Weeds

Herbicides

The testing of herbicides has resulted in materials that are effective and less expensive. The list of recommended herbicides changes continually as more effective materials are approved for use and as others become unavailable. Therefore, this bulletin makes no recommendations of specific herbicides and only uses herbicides currently available to illustrate methods of control (see reference 9).

Formulations

The pure chemical compounds are not usually effective or easy to use. They are made more useful by manufacturers by combining them with other materials in a formulation. The chemical can be adsorbed on clay, vermiculite, or other suitable materials and applied as granules. Application of granules to foliage is best done early in the morning when the granules stick to

the dew on the weed leaves. For soil application the granules are applied to dry foliage so that they fall through the leaves to the ground. Moisture is necessary to spread and activate the herbicide and hasten weed seed germination.

For spring application the chemical compound may be a soluble liquid or powder that readily mixes with water. It may be an emulsifiable concentrate that readily disperses in water forming a milky substance. Some chemicals are made into a finely ground powder that is not soluble, but is easily wetted by and dispersed in water; this type of mixture must be agitated for the particles to stay in suspension and be spread evenly.

Time of Application

Preplant treatments are applied before planting when there is little danger to the turfgrass. Soil fumigants are applied to the soil with water to kill underground plant parts, including seeds, roots, and stems.

Preemergence herbicides are applied to the soil surface to prevent weed seedlings from getting started. Once the seedlings have passed a certain stage of development, the treatment may no longer be effective. Applying recommended preemergence herbicides to a lawn when forsythia is in bloom prevents crabgrass seedlings from developing. Too early an application lessens the effect, and too late a treatment may not get the seedling in time and may result in a lawn full of crabgrass.

Postemergence herbicides are applied to foliage of actively growing weeds. The control may be by direct contact on the leaves or by the herbicide moving in the plant.

Check the herbicide label to see what the optimum time is for treatment to secure the best results at the least cost and with the least injury to desirable plants.

Systemic Herbicides

Some chemicals only affect the part of a plant that is directly touched (contact). A systemic herbicide is one that is absorbed by leaves or roots and moves through the plant, affecting areas distant from the point of contact and often the entire plant. Systemic herbicides control growing crabgrass and yellow nutsedge. Systemics must be applied at the proper concentration to be effective. Too high a concentration may injure tissue; as a result movement through the plant is prevented. Too low a concentration may not be effective, but repeated applications at low rates may be most effective.

Herbicide Selectivity

Most of the herbicides we use on turf weeds are effective at specific rates on certain weeds with no injury to grass. This differential effect is called selectivity. For example, an herbicide such as 2,4-D sprayed on a lawn eliminates dandelions and plantains, may not be very effective on white clover, and usually does not injure mature turfgrass. Bluegrass seedlings are easily injured until large enough to have been mowed two to three times. Many herbicides may be safe on turfgrass, but are definitely not safe on nongrassy ornamentals, vegetables, and other plants.

Safety

Check the herbicide label for the safest, most effective time to apply herbicides. If used according to directions on the package, herbicides should not be a hazard to people, pets, turfgrass, and other desirable plants in the garden or landscape. Do not use at rates above those recommended. It is best to use phenoxy herbicides, such as 2,4-D, MCPP, and the like, in early spring and late fall when temperatures are lower and there is less foliage of desirable plants exposed. Do not use a sprayer for growth regulator herbicides, such as 2,4-D, on any plants other than grass. Use another sprayer for controlling insects, diseases, and weeds in the garden. Handle all pesticides with care and read the directions on the label for special precautions.

Summary

To minimize weed problems—

- select the recommended grass for your site;
- plant your new lawn in the fall;
- use adequate fertilizer (and lime or sulfur if needed), especially when starting a new lawn;
- mow your lawn at least 1 1/2 inches high to reduce weed competition;
- control diseases and insects that damage turf and allow weed encroachment;
- water the lawn frequently but thoroughly, not too little too often;
- consult the *Home Lawns: Grass Varieties and Pest Control Guide* for the list of current weed control measures;
- follow label directions and precautions on specific amounts and timing when using herbicides.

Diseases

Unhealthy and dead grass in a home lawn can be caused by a number of factors. Diseases caused by specific living organisms, usually fungi, are only one of many factors to be considered in maintaining an aesthetically pleasing and durable lawn. Other factors involved in the establishment and maintenance of a good lawn, as discussed earlier in this publication, are prerequisites for growing good turfgrass. No amount of disease control effort can overcome poor growing conditions or improper maintenance practices. Diseases are more likely to occur when lawns have been improperly established or maintained. By altering some management practices, you can appreciably retard disease development. Inadequate soil aeration, overwatering, poor drainage, improper fertilization, and mowing too low may all lead to disease problems.

Turfgrass injuries from other causes are frequently confused with symptoms of turf diseases. Drought injury, for instance, may resemble disease. In many cases drought occurs where thin layers of soil lie over buried debris such as rocks, lumber, plaster, and concrete. The soil dries rapidly in hot summer weather. Dead spots or patches that suddenly appear in a lawn may be caused by fertilizer burn, dog urine, spilled fuel oil, gasoline, oil and grease, exhaust heat from power mowers, or improper use of herbicides and insecticides.

Mowing practices can cause a diseaselike condition as well as influence the actual development of disease. Cutting grass too closely, called scalping, or using a mower with dull blades may result in a condition that looks like disease. Infrequent mowing, which produces excessive clippings in a mat, may encourage disease in the hot, humid environment under the mat. Grass weakened by frequent low mowing often appears off-color and is more susceptible to disease.

Diseases in a home lawn are often difficult to diagnose until the symptoms are obvious and the disease is in an advanced state. Disease symptoms vary in type and degree, depending on the variety of grass in the lawn. Some varieties have resistance to some diseases, but no variety is resistant to all turfgrass diseases. For the latest list of disease-resistant varieties, see *Home Lawns: Grass Varieties and Pest Control Guide* (reference 9). Diseases on susceptible grass varieties can usually be controlled with chemicals called fungicides. These materials are applied with a sprayer or a spreader, or they can be incorporated with a fertilizer. The frequency of fungicide application depends on weather conditions, the disease to be controlled, grass variety, cultural practices, and the degree of perfection desired by the homeowner. Disease control materials are toxic and should be stored, handled, and used with proper precautions.

Snow mold

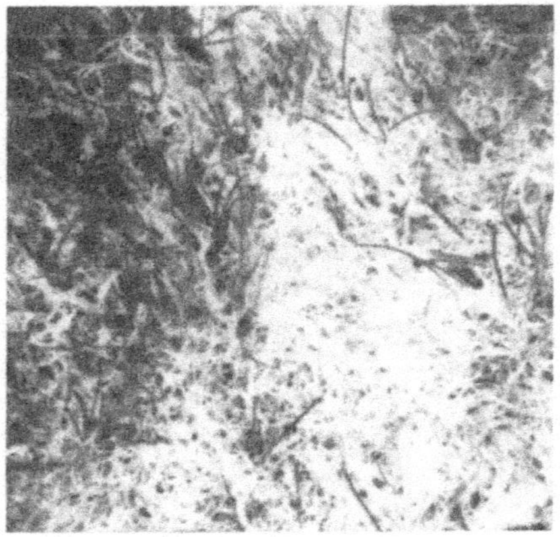

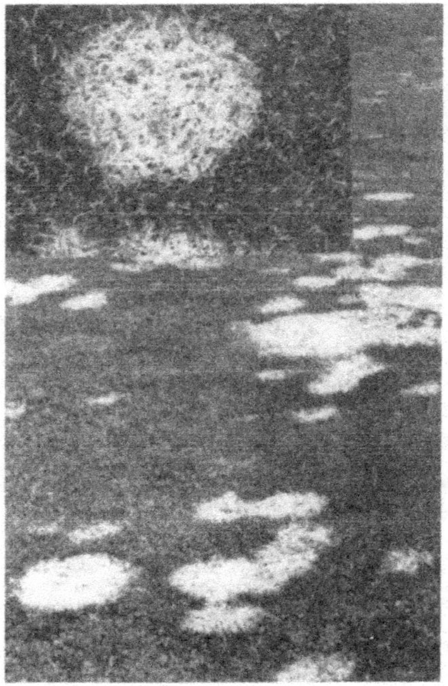

Snow Mold

Snow mold is the first disease to appear on a lawn in late winter or early spring. Snow mold diseases may occur on home lawns when temperatures are in the 32° to 45° F range and very moist conditions prevail. This is frequently the case under a snow cover during a thaw period. Spots of dead grass varying from an inch to several feet in diameter occur. The fungus growing in the spots gives the grass a grayish-white or pinkish appearance.

Snow mold can be lessened by fertilization practices that do not leave the grass in a lush growing stage as winter begins. Continue mowing in late fall so that long grass (which has a tendency to mat down) is not present. Snow mold is usually not a serious problem for the home lawn. Effective chemical controls must be applied before the first lasting snow falls.

Leaf Spot

Leaf spot is one of the most destructive lawn diseases. Leaf spot disease usually attacks lawns during periods of cool, moist weather in spring or fall. The first stage of the disease appears on the leaves as straw-colored spots with reddish-brown to black borders. In the second stage (melting-out) the stems, crowns, and roots become

Leaf spot

discolored and rot. It is important to diagnose leaf spot and spray for its control during the first stage of the disease. Extensive damage may result if the disease is permitted to proceed to the second stage. Most varieties of Kentucky bluegrass are resistant to this disease, and many fine fescues are susceptible. Mowing at 1 1/2- to 2 1/2-inch heights and using lower than usual rates of nitrogen fertilizers (in early spring) may decrease the damage from leaf spot. Those lawns that have exhibited severe leaf spot occurrence should not be fertilized until the weather becomes warm and dry in late spring.

Dollar Spot

Dollar spot disease may appear on lawns as straw-colored areas 2 to 6 inches in diameter. These areas may coalesce to form larger dead patches. Close inspection of the leaf blade reveals bleached areas across the width of the leaf and tan borders above and below the lesion. This disease is most prevalent during summer when hot days are followed by cool nights. Dollar spot seldom damages turf permanently, but it may lead to increased weed encroachment. The disease is more active when nitrogen fertilization has been inadequate and the soil is dry.

Dollar spot

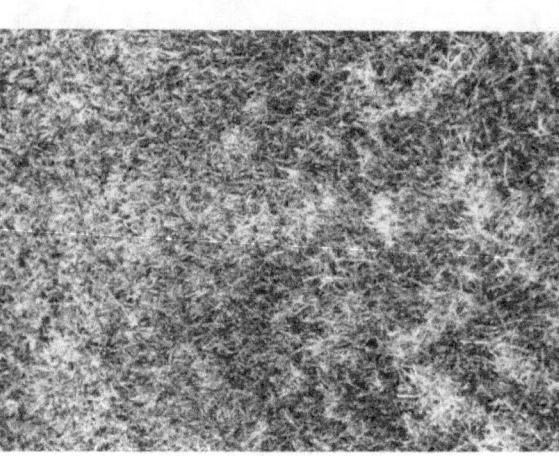

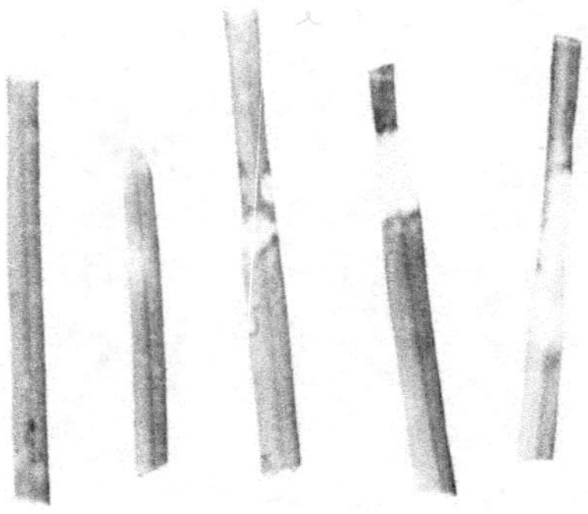

Brown Patch

Brown patch is most likely to occur in summer during periods of hot, humid weather. Lawns of any grass variety may be attacked, and the affected areas appear as brown patches a few inches to several feet in diameter. A severe attack leaves bare spots where the turf is killed. High nitrogen fertilization favors the occurrence of this disease. Watering early in the day to allow the grass to dry before night also helps to prevent this disease.

Pythium Blight or Damping-off

Pythium blight is most troublesome during hot weather on poorly drained areas. The diseased patches often follow shapes of the wettest areas. Plants are killed and feel slimy or greasy in the early morning. The *Pythium* fungus is especially apt to attack young, newly seeded grasses; a disease known as damping-off results. This disease is less troublesome if you plant seeds in the fall or early enough in the spring to allow the grass plants to mature before hot weather begins. Avoid overwatering the seedling turf. Standing water and hot weather encourage damping-off.

Rust

Rust may be found on lawn grasses in late summer or fall. A heavy attack causes the turf to have a reddish brown cast because of pinhead-sized pustules on the leaves. The brown, powdery spores can be wiped from the leaf. Rust is frequently a problem on some Kentucky bluegrasses and on all perennial ryegrasses. Fungicides can be applied to eliminate rust soon after it has appeared. Adequate fertilization and good watering help to reduce rust damage to a lawn.

Powdery Mildew

Powdery mildew usually appears during moist weather in summer or in shaded areas of a lawn. The disease can be identified from the white powder that can be wiped from the leaf blades. Powdery mildew usually is not a serious problem, but a mildew fungicide can be used, if desired, to eradicate the disease after it has appeared. Any management practices that reduce shading of the grass and increase the air movement help to reduce mildew disease. Some grass varieties that are particularly shade tolerant and are resistant to this disease have been developed and are recommended.

Stripe smut

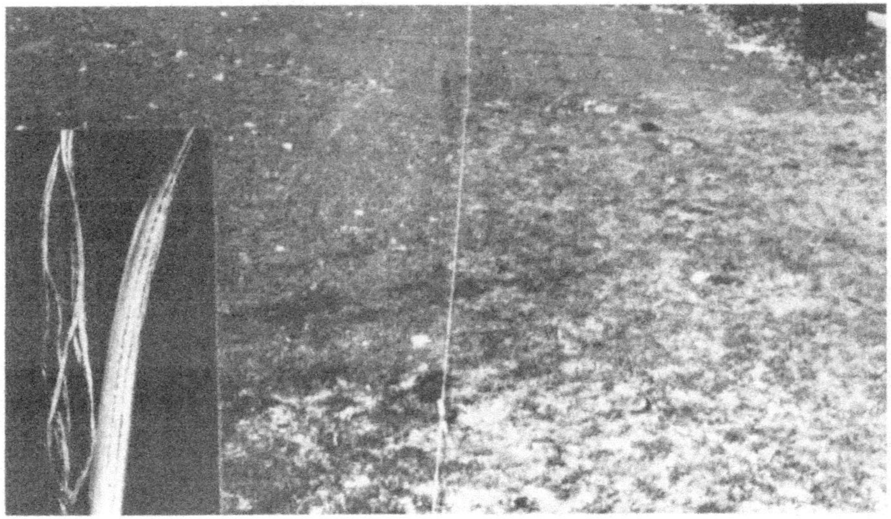

Stripe Smut

Stripe smut may be a problem on Kentucky bluegrass lawns. The infected grass has the general appearance of poor growth, and close inspection of the leaf blade reveals gray or black longitudinal stripes caused by the fungus growing inside the leaf blade. When the stripes rupture, the black, powdery spores are released, and the leaf dries and dies. A white cloth rubbed over the grass becomes discolored by the black spores. Symptoms are most noticeable in late spring and early fall. Fungicide treatments help to control this disease, but must be applied in the early spring or late fall.

Fusarium blight of Kent bluegrass

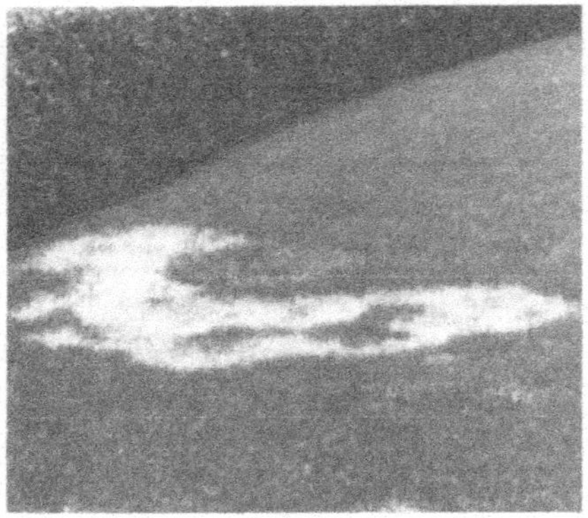

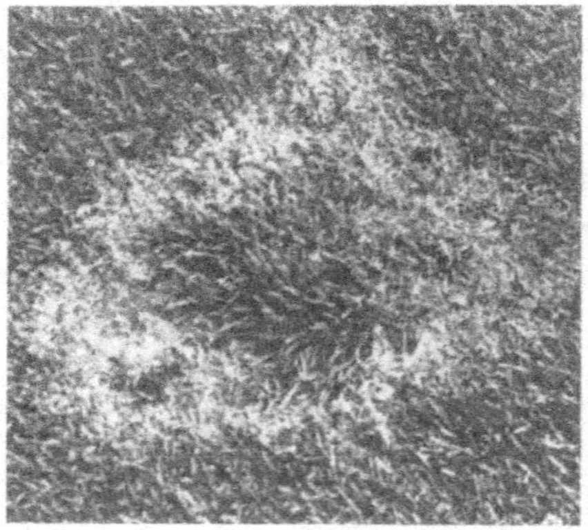

Fusarium Blight

Fusarium blight occurs mainly on Kentucky bluegrasses. It is most prevalent during periods of high temperatures in July and August. Frequently the first symptoms appear on turf along walkways and driveways. Sometimes an island of unaffected grass will remain in the center of the diseased patch, giving its charactertistic "frog-eye" appearance. On individual leaves the infected tissue fades to light straw color and is without a distinctive border. In dealing with this disease it is important to keep the grass in a healthy, vigorous condition. Adequate, but not excessive, fertilization and watering practices are important. Any cultural practice that weakens or places a stress on the grass makes it more vulnerable to this disease. Fungicide controls must be applied before the onset of the disease. Effective treatments should be started in early June.

Red thread: D, red threads protruding from tips of diseased grass blades; H, healthy grass blades.

Fairy Ring

Many kinds of fungi growing in a lawn can produce a condition known as a fairy ring. This disease appears in the spring as circular bands of dark green grass. The grass on the inner side of the ring often dies. The rings will enlarge each year and may achieve large diameters. In late summer, mushrooms may develop in some rings. There is no adequate control for this disease. Aeration of the soil in the compacted ring area is advised. Symptoms can be masked by an early spring application of a soluble nitrogen fertilizer, adequate watering, and frequent fertilization.

Red Thread

Red thread or pink patch disease occurs on perennial ryegrasses and fine fescues and somewhat less on Kentucky bluegrasses. The disease affects small patches of grass, which can coalesce to cover large areas when the disease is severe. On humid nights a pink fungal layer may cover leaf blades, or a pink to red fungal strand (red thread) may grow from the end of blighted leaves. The disease is reduced by adequate nitrogen fertilizer and watering. Fungicides may be required for controlling this disease on some grasses.

Disease Control

A satisfactory home lawn often can be maintained with only a little attention to disease control. The amount of effort spent on the control of lawn diseases depends on the excellence of the turf desired and on the seriousness of the disease threat. Cultural practices that encourage a vigorous, hardy turf help minimize both the occurrence of turf diseases and the necessity for control measures. Proper control of a turf disease starts with proper identification of the problem. Early disease diagnosis makes control easier. Table 7 provides a key to help in identifying common lawn diseases. Alternatively, contact your local Cooperative Extension agent for assistance.

Chemical control is justified when diseases become severe and when they reoccur on the lawn each year. Fungicides are often effective in curing a disease soon after the disease is first observed. Curative control is best for controlling leaf spot, dollar spot, brown patch, rust, powdery mildew, and red thread. For other diseases such as snow mold, stripe smut, and fusarium blight, the chemicals must be applied before disease symptoms appear. This approach is called preventive control.

A simplified preventive spray program to control most lawn diseases would include an early spring, late spring, and late fall application of a fungicide. Recommendations for specific problems can be found in *Home Lawns: Grass Varieties and Pest Control Guide* (reference 9). All fungicides are limited in the number of diseases they control; proper selection is, therefore, very important. Once the grasses are dead, chemicals will not bring them back to life. But the fungicides do promote the growth of healthy new grass blades. Where death is extensive, reseed the dead areas and be alert for early symptoms the following year.

Table 7. Key to common diseases of lawn grasses

(Choose between each pair of numbered statements the one that better fits the observed condition. Then proceed to the number referred to and make another choice. Continue until the disease is named.)

0.	Young grass seedlings collapse or seed does not germinate	Damping off; seed rot
0.	Disease is present on mature grass stand	*See* 1
1.	Disease occurs in winter or cold weather	*See* 2
1.	Disease occurs in spring, summer, or fall	*See* 3
2.	White to pinkish fungal growth on leaves; later the patches of dead leaves are matted and whitish gray	Fusarium patch (pink snow mold)
2.	White to black halo of fungal growth surrounds young patch; dead leaves are tan and crowns often contain tan, red, brown, or black spherical growths	Typhula blight (gray snow mold)
3.	Diseases often of general occurrence rather than in distinct patches	*See* 4
3.	Diseases occur mostly in distinct patches; patches may coalesce	*See* 12
4.	Leaves with distinctly outlined spots	*See* 5
4.	Leaves without distinct spots, but colored fungal growth visible	*See* 8
5.	Spots mostly found in midleaf	*See* 6
5.	Spots in midleaf or leaf ends blighted	*See* 7
6.	Straw-colored leaf spots with reddish black borders; predominant in cool, moist weather	Helminthosporium leaf spot
6.	Straw-colored spots with dark brown margins across entire leaf	Dollar spot
7.	Leaf spots variable; leaf ends may be blighted; tiny black spherical fungal growths may be in dead leaf	Ascochyta, septoria, and other leaf spots
7.	As above, but small black spines emerge from blighted leaves	Anthracnose
8.	Fungal growth pink, red, or reddish brown	*See* 9
8.	Fungal growth white, gray, or black	*See* 10
9.	Red to reddish brown pustules on leaf	Rust
9.	Tiny pink to red fungal threads on ends of dead leaves	Red thread
10.	Gray to black spherical growths on outside of leaf	Slime mold
10.	Fungal growth visible inside leaf or flat on surface	*See* 11
11.	Gray to black stripes between leaf veins; or leaf may be shredded	Stripe smut
11.	White fungal mats over part or all of leaf	Powdery mildew
12.	Small to large patches (6 in. to many feet in diameter)	*See* 13
12.	Mostly small patches (less than 6- to 12-in. diameter)	*See* 15
13.	Circular patch of living grass surrounded by adjacent rings of stimulated and depressed (or dead) grass; mushrooms may occur	Fairy ring

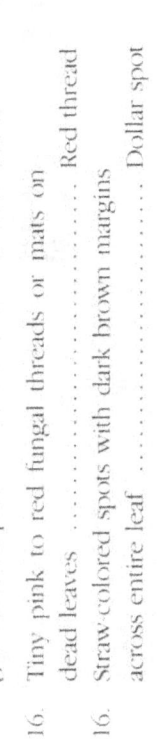

13. Irregularly shaped patches without a ring of stimulated grass .... *See* 14
14. Dying grass surrounded by gray ring in morning; hot, humid weather .... Brown patch
14. Patches in thinned turf; helminthosporium leaf spot and rotted stems present .... Melting-out
15. Fungal growth or bordered leaf lesions on grass around patches .... *See* 16
15. Indistinctly bordered lesions or no lesions on grass around patches .... *See* 17
16. Tiny pink to red fungal threads or mats on dead leaves .... Red thread
16. Straw-colored spots with dark brown margins across entire leaf .... Dollar spot
17. Circular, crescent, or doughnut-shaped dead patches in full sun; irregularly shaped leaf lesions are straw colored and without distinct borders .... Fusarium blight
17. Small patches of blackened, greasy-feeling leaves intertwined by cottony fungal growth in early morning; reddish brown patches of matted leaves later in day; patches coalesce to form streaks in low areas; hot, humid weather .... Pythium blight

NOTE: Damage due to insects feeding on grass plants may resemble disease damage. Frequently, the responsible insects or wormlike grubs can be found by careful examination of the thatch and upper soil layer in damaged areas.

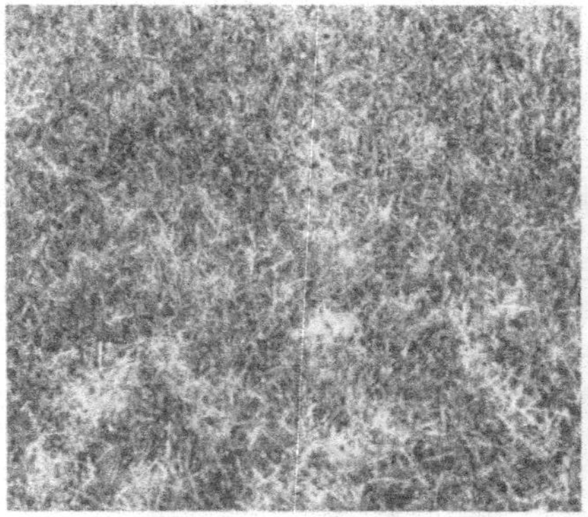

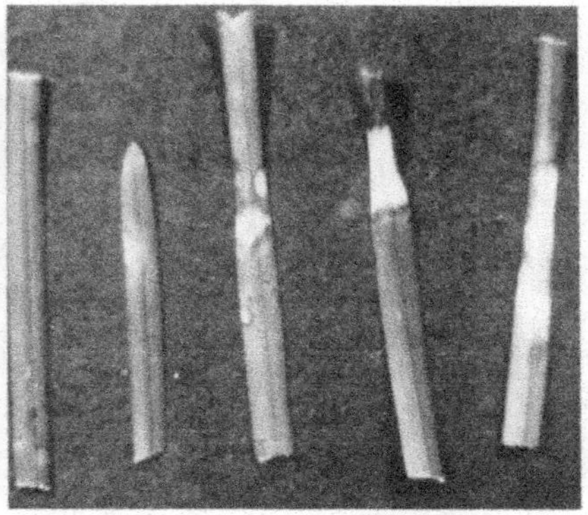

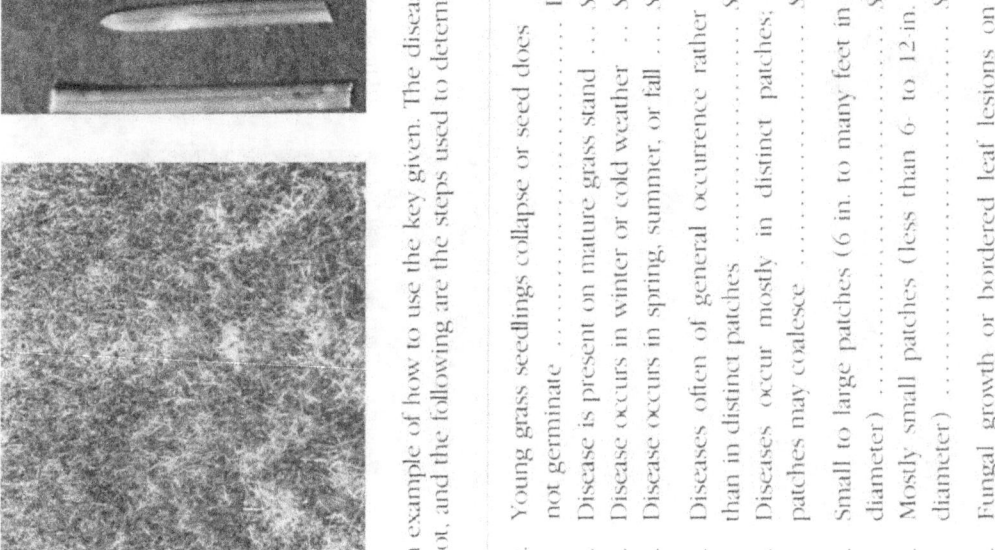

An example of how to use the key given. The disease shown above is dollar spot, and the following are the steps used to determine the disease:

0. Young grass seedlings collapse or seed does not germinate .... Damping-off; seed rot
0. Disease is present on mature grass stand ... *See* 1
1. Disease occurs in winter or cold weather .. *See* 2
1. Disease occurs in spring, summer, or fall ... *See* 3

3. Diseases often of general occurrence rather than in distinct patches .... *See* 4
3. Diseases occur mostly in distinct patches; patches may coalesce .... *See* 12

12. Small to large patches (6 in. to many feet in diameter) .... *See* 13
12. Mostly small patches (less than 6- to 12-in. diameter) .... *See* 15

15. Fungal growth or bordered leaf lesions on grass around patches .... *See* 16
15. Indistinctly bordered lesions or no lesions on grass around patches .... *See* 17

16. Tiny pink to red fungal threads or mats on dead leaves .... Red thread
16. Straw-colored spots with dark brown margins across entire leaf .... Dollar spot

Insects

Certain scarab grubs and other turf pests are serious in many areas of New York State. The Japanese beetle has spread to most city and suburban lawns throughout the state except in the northern-most counties. The oriental beetle is as destructive as the Japanese beetle in southeastern New York. The European chafer is gradually spreading and is now serious throughout most of the state. Other grubs, such as Asiatic garden beetle and masked chafer, are often troublesome in the southeastern part of the state. Chinch bugs and sod webworms were previously regarded as turf-grass pests of southeastern New York, but are now serious pests of many areas of upstate New York. The bluegrass billbug is a lawn pest that may be found anywhere in New York.

Insect-damaged lawns may yellow, look thinned out or ragged, and become brown when irregular patches of grass are killed. In areas where grubs are known to be present, you should look for them and protect lawn areas before serious damage occurs. You can be sure it is insect damage only if you find the insects.

Mature scarab grub, the most destructive stage

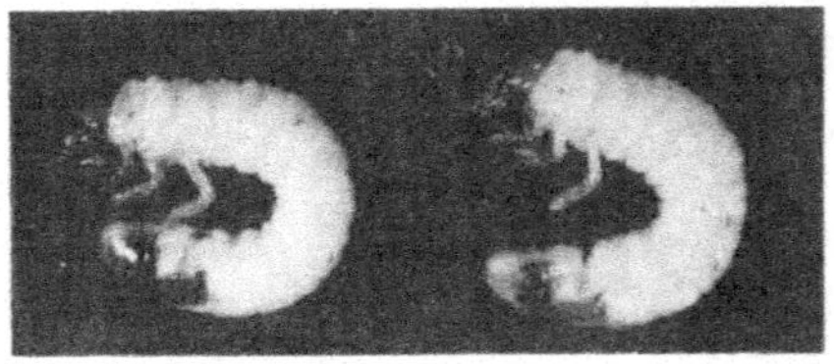

Grubs

Scarab larvae chew off grass roots. Seriously grub-damaged turf can easily be pulled because of the lack of roots. In September and October and again in April to early June, the grubs can be found easily and quickly under the loose sod. Grubs are white, wormlike insects with brown heads and three pairs of legs near the head end. They are **C** shaped and may be from 1/2 to 1 inch long, but are smallest in late summer when still young. Grub injury is most often worst in sunny areas. Symptoms appear as wilted turf occurring after the ground dries out in late spring or early fall. In an area where you suspect grub damage, dig a square foot sample of sod to a depth of 3 inches. Pick apart the sod over a piece of cardboard and examine the soil carefully. If there are five or more grubs under any square foot, treat the soil immediately. Remember that during midsummer there are no grubs, because the insects are in the adult stage. One indication of a potential grub problem is the obvious heavy flight of adult beetles.

Mid-July through August is the most effective treatment period on annual grub problem areas. It is much easier to control grubs during this period because they are small. During very late fall, winter, and early spring, grubs are much deeper down in the soil and cannot be controlled easily. Make sure the soil is moist before treatment to encourage grub feeding near the soil surface. It is not necessary to know which species of beetle grub is present to apply effective control measures at this time. All species of grubs can be treated in April.

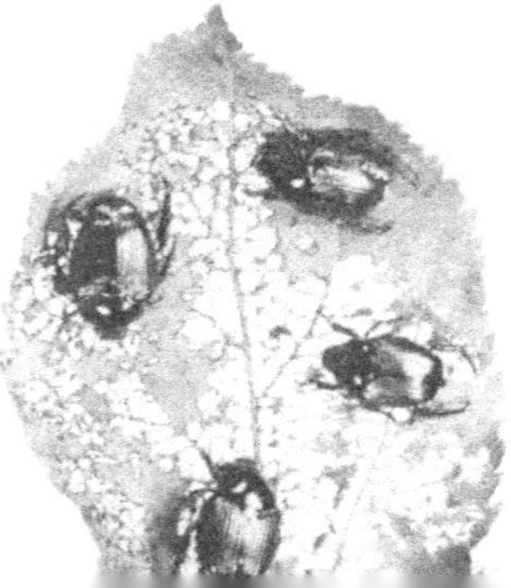

An adult scarab, the Japanese beetle

Turf easily lifted as a result of scarab grub feeding

Bluegrass billbug larvae, the destructive stage

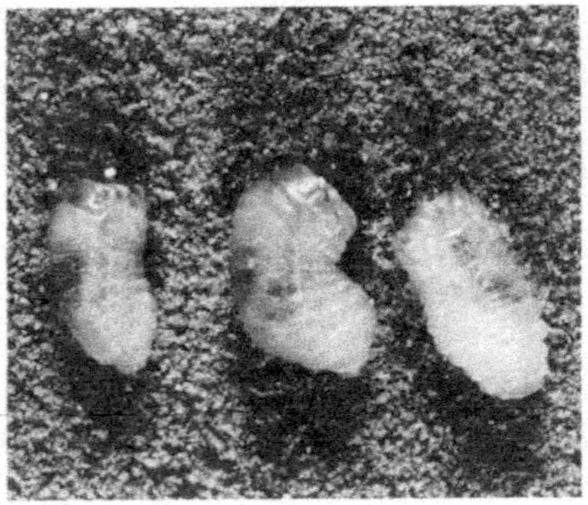

Bluegrass Billbug

Bluegrass billbug adults (weevils) are black, about 5/16 inch long, and have a prominent snout. Billbugs can be seen walking over driveways and sidewalks adjacent to lawns during warm sunny days of early spring and summer. This provides a warning of possible lawn destruction later. If one or two adult weevils are observed within a minute's search, treatment should be applied immediately to kill the adults before further egg laying occurs. Adults feed on the grass stems near the base of the plant, but cause only minor damage. Eggs and larvae are present in the same areas. Destruction of lawns occurs when the larger grubs feed on the crowns of the grass plants and cause weakening and death of large patches of grass during late June into August. The brown-headed, white legless grubs are about 1/4 inch long when mature and can be found within an inch or two of the soil surface. The presence of frass, which resembles fine sawdust, around the crowns is characteristic of their activity. Treatments should be made to arrest further lawn damage, although treatment at this time is not so effective as killing the adults.

Chinch Bugs, Sod Webworms, and Cutworms

Chinch bugs, sod webworms, and cutworms feed on the leaves and stems of the grass, not on the roots as do the grubs. They do not occur in the soil but above or on the soil surface. Treatments for these insects may be required even though grub control methods have been used. Applications for these pests must be made to the grass rather than to the soil.

Chinch bugs cause yellowing and subsequent browning of the grass, usually in gradually enlarging patches. Damage is most likely to be seen during June to August. Chinch bugs are active earlier in the year and should be controlled when first seen. Populations build up in thick turf, particularly in bentgrass. Adult chinch bugs are very small, about 1/5 inch long, and black. Young nymphs are red or brown and black, measuring 1/8 inch in length. By examining the grass closely at ground level, you can find the tiny bugs. There are two methods to test for chinch bugs: (1) Select a sunny spot along the border of the yellowed or suspected area of your lawn. Cut out both ends of a large tin can and push one end of the can about 2 inches into the sod. Then fill the can with water nearly to the top. If chinch bugs are present, they will float to the surface of the water in about 5 minutes. (2) Place a 1-foot square piece of white cloth over the suspected area of the lawn and thoroughly flood the sod beneath it. If chinch bugs are present, they will crawl up on the cloth in about 5 minutes. If several are found, treatment is necessary.

Bluegrass billbug adult

Hairy chinch bug adult and nymphs

Sod webworms, feed on blades, stems, and crowns

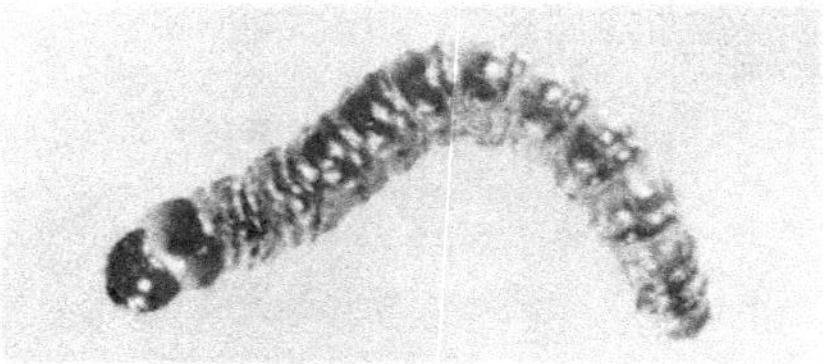

Moths of sod webworms may be seen during cloudy days and at dusk of hot summer days. As you walk across the lawn, the moths fly ahead of you a short distance in a zig-zag pattern before alighting. They drop their eggs over the lawn during their nightly flights. As eggs hatch, young worms feed on grass blades; but as they grow larger, they feed on blades, stems, and even the crowns of grasses. Worms feed only at night and rest in silk-lined tunnels during the day. Small yellow spots of damaged grass coalesce with other spots; eventually, large areas of grass may turn brown and die. Cutworms also feed during the night and cause similar yellow spots, which may coalesce to form large patches of dead grass. If large numbers of webworm moths are seen flying over the lawn during the evening, insecticides should be applied within a week or two at the most. If yellowing of grass occurs and worms and green masses of fecal pellets are found in silken tunnels on the ground or in the thatch, either webworms or cutworms may be present, and treatment should be started immediately.

Sod webworm moths, stage most readily seen

Ants, Earthworms, and Other Insects

Neither ants nor earthworms are damaging to the grass itself, but may spoil the appearance of a good lawn by the mounds of earth thrown up as they tunnel into the soil. Wasps or hornets also may nest in lawns, especially on lighter or sandy soils. They cause little damage to the grass, but may be objectionable because of the danger of stinging. For specific control methods see *Home Lawns: Grass Varieties and Pest Control Guide.*

Improving a Poor Lawn

An old, established lawn that has been neglected for years is sometimes easy to repair. First, control weeds that are competing with the turfgrass for nutrients and water. Refer to the weed section for further details. Second, make sure the pH is in the proper range. Third, fertilize at least three times during the first season. In many cases proper fertilization will dramatically improve the quality of a poor lawn. Fourth, water to avoid drought stress. Fifth, mow at the proper height and frequency. Most older lawns often need no more than these simple, inexpensive steps to provide a beautiful lawn within a few years.

At the other extreme is the lawn that contains only scattered patches of turfgrass with many bare and (or) weed areas. This may have been caused by poor drainage, poor soil, the wrong kind of turfgrass for your site, improper maintenance practices, crabgrass and other weed infestation, insect and disease damage, and other problems.

Renovating a Poor Lawn

If your lawn contains at least 50 percent of desirable turfgrass in a fairly uniform stand, a thorough renovation may save it. However, if more than 50 percent of the lawn contains undesirable turfgrasses or is in weeds, especially weeds like quackgrass, yellow nutsedge, bentgrass, or annual bluegrass, consider starting all over and reestablishing the lawn. Remember you must include a nonselective herbicide treatment to control all undesirable weeds and any remaining turfgrass.

Lawn renovation should *only* be done in late summer to early fall, usually from August 15 to September 1. Plan ahead by taking a soil sample in June and have it tested for pH and nutrient content. The results may help explain the cause(s) of your poor lawn and help eliminate similar problems in the future.

The first step in lawn renovation is to remove undesirable weeds. Annual grassy weeds such as crabgrass and goosegrass will die after the first frost and, therefore, may not be worth controlling. The two types of weeds that need to be controlled are broad-leaved and perennial grassy weeds. Refer to the weed control section for further details.

You must wait at least 2 weeks after applying a nonselective herbicide before proceeding any further. This allows the herbicide to totally kill the weeds and also reduces the chance of injuring the turfgrass seedlings. At this time, you can rake the bare areas to remove any debris and loosen the soil. A power dethatching machine can also be used for this purpose.

One of the most important and overlooked steps in lawn renovation is applying enough fertilizer. It is essential to apply 2 pounds of actual nitrogen per 1,000 square feet in establishing a new lawn. Use a complete fertilizer with a ratio of 1:1:1 or similar ratio. Refer to table 4 for the specific amount of fertilizer required. If the soil test results indicated the pH was below 6.0 or above 7.5, apply ground limestone or elemental sulfur at the amount recommended.

Your lawn is now ready for seeding or sodding. If the bare spots are small and evenly distributed throughout the lawn, broadcast the seed over the entire area.

However, if the bare spots are confined to large patches, only seed those areas. The seed must have good contact with the soil to germinate and grow. A slicer-seeder machine is well suited for this purpose. Lawns that contain a lot of thatch are difficult to reseed. Therefore, the thatch should be removed before seeding.

If possible, carefully rake the seed into the surface 1/8 inch of soil and lightly roll the entire area to help ensure good seed-soil contact. As with any seeding it is important to properly water, mow, and fertilize. Follow the methods outlined in the postplanting section for these operations.

Lawns in the Shade

Shaded lawns are troublesome because of reduced light and competition with trees for water and nutrients. Even the most shade-tolerant grasses never make as good a sod in the shade as grasses growing in the sun.

Sometimes shade alone is the chief difficulty such as on sites near buildings or under deep-rooted, high-branched trees. In many cases good soil preparation plus a shade-tolerant turfgrass mixture makes for an acceptable lawn. It has been found that fine fescues are the best grasses to use if the soil is dry, or rough bluegrasses, if the soil is moist. Under trees with about 60 percent shade where some sunlight streams through, several shade-tolerant Kentucky bluegrasses do well. Refer to *Home Lawns: Grass Varieties and Pest Control Guide* (reference 9) for specific varieties.

Under dense, shallow-rooted trees, the turfgrass has a much harder time, because trees cut off the light and rob the soil of water and fertilizer. Of the common trees, Norway maple is the worst offender. In such situations even your best efforts to establish a lawn may fail. Give your new lawn every advantage. This means special care in all details of planting. Fertilize lightly spring and fall and mow at 2 inches or higher. Also do not overwater. In many cases, deep feeding and watering of trees can help improve your lawn.

If your best efforts fail and you still want a lawn, try ryegrass. Use perennial ryegrass at the rate of 6 to 8 pounds per 1,000 square feet instead of the other grasses. Mow it high, water whenever the soil is dry, and fertilize each spring and fall. Whenever dead patches appear, loosen the soil and sow more seed.

If you are unable to grow a lawn, you must look for a lawn substitute or ground covers suitable for your area. If these also fail, consider flagstone, brick, or gravel.

Steep Slopes

Avoid steep slopes whenever possible. They tend to be dry, and lawns are difficult to establish and maintain. If you have a steep slope and decide to use turfgrass, be sure to round off the crest of the slope to avoid scalping.

Whenever possible, sod a steep slope. You avoid the chance of a heavy rainfall washing away all the topsoil. Also, sodding generally ensures that the slope will become established. On very steep slopes, each piece of sod may need to be fastened with a peg and twine. Follow the sodding procedure described previously.

To plant a slope with seed, be careful not to skip any of the important points described for seeding. Pay special attention to seedbed preparation and fertilizing and be sure to plant in early fall. A straw mulch, burlap, or cheesecloth covering is essential during the first few weeks of establishment. Give turf on steep slopes the same care as other lawn areas and remember to fertilize, mow, and water properly.

Ground covers such as crown vetch may be used as substitutes for turf on steep slopes. Consult your local Cooperative Extension agent for assistance in selecting a suitable substitute for turfgrass on steep slopes.

Turfgrasses and Substitutes to Avoid

For lawn use in New York State, avoid the following plants: Mondo, Dichondra, pearlwort, St. Augustinegrass, Bahiagrass, and Bermudagrass.

In midsummer, a good sod of zoysias (*Zoisia japonica* and *Z. matrella*) is superior to that of unirrigated cool-season grasses. It is more durable to summer traffic; is more tolerant of low fertility, heat, drought, close cutting, and summer

Table 8. Materials and rates used to control moss

Material	*Amount/1,000 sq ft*
Copper sulfate*	2–3 oz
Superphosphate	2–3 lb
Ferrous sulfate*	1–3 oz

*Mix in 2–3 gal water, then apply.

weed invasion; and requires a bit less mowing. These advantages are especially noteworthy in Meyer zoysia, a selection of *Z. japonica*. Accompanying disadvantages are that the zoysias turn straw brown in autumn and remain so until mid to late spring. They are not resistant to traffic or weed invasion when dormant, must be started from plugs or sprigs of sod, and are not tolerant of shady conditions. It takes several years of patience to produce a solid sod of zoysia, which has not been consistently winter-hardy in New York State. In addition, a severe outbreak of chinch bug can totally destroy a zoysia lawn in one season.

Hobbyists may find trial plantings of zoysia interesting. This may be especially true on Long Island or in similar situations where turf is desired and used only in summer. Zoysia is unlikely to satisfy the desire for a troublefree carefree lawn in New York.

Moss

Moss is an indication that growing conditions are not ideal for turfgrass and often occurs under shaded conditions. Moss does not "crowd" the grasses; it merely occupies spaces where grass has not survived. Improving the conditions for the lawn, in many cases, drives out the moss. Sometimes poor drainage is the reason for moss to prevail; therefore, improve the drainage before you take other measures. In some cases lime may be needed (test the soil), but lime without fertilizer is seldom helpful. Rake off the moss with an iron rake and follow the renovation program suggested earlier. Carry on with routine proper maintenance practices, and the moss problem will gradually disappear.

Several chemicals have been found to control moss, but it is important to correct the cause of the problem. Use these materials at recommended rates (see table 8) when all other methods fail. Under certain circumstances repeat treatment may be necessary.

Moles, Skunks, and Other Animals

Moles raise ridges in the lawn as they burrow through the soil in search of grubs and earthworms to eat. Grubproofing your lawn will decrease mole troubles. If moles persist, try a mole trap.

Skunks may dig holes in your lawn in search of grubs and earthworms. Their activities often indicate the need for grubproofing. Once the grubs are killed, the skunks usually go elsewhere. Refer to the insect section for further details on grub control.

Calculations for Home Lawn Practices

You must be able to determine the area of your lawn if proper applications of fertilizer, lime or sulfur, and pesticides are to be made. Follow the given formulas to determine the area of your lawn.

Area of a Square or Rectangle

Area = L × W
L = length
W = width

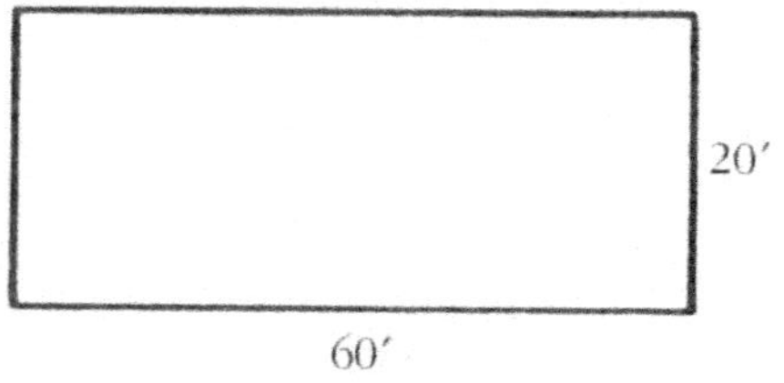

Area = 60′ × 20′ = 1,200 square feet

Area of a Circle

Area = ΠR^2
Π = 3.14
R = radius

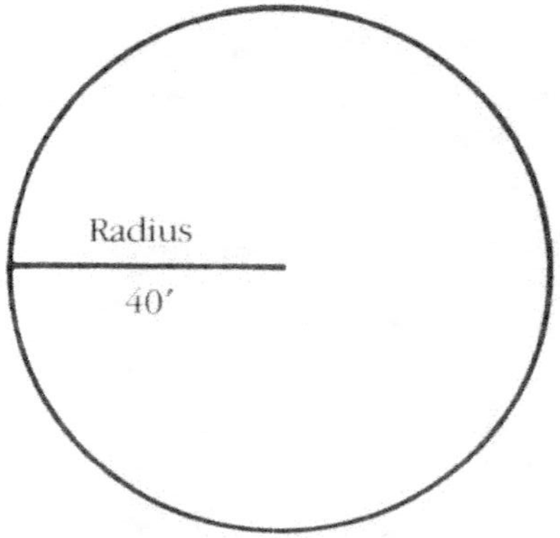

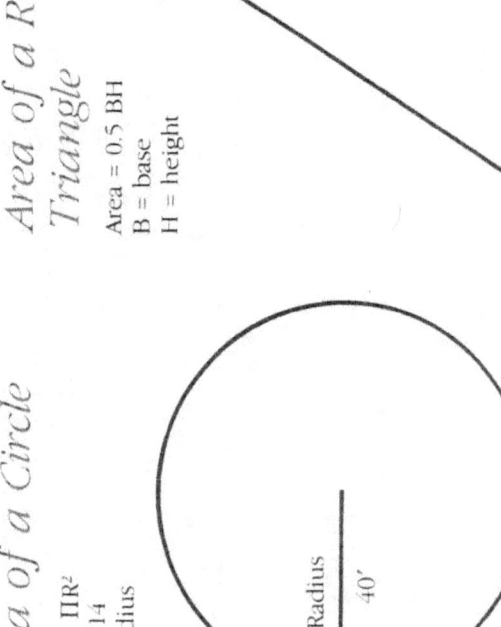

Area = 3.14 × 40′ × 40′
Area = 5,024 square feet

Area = 0.8 D^2
D = diameter

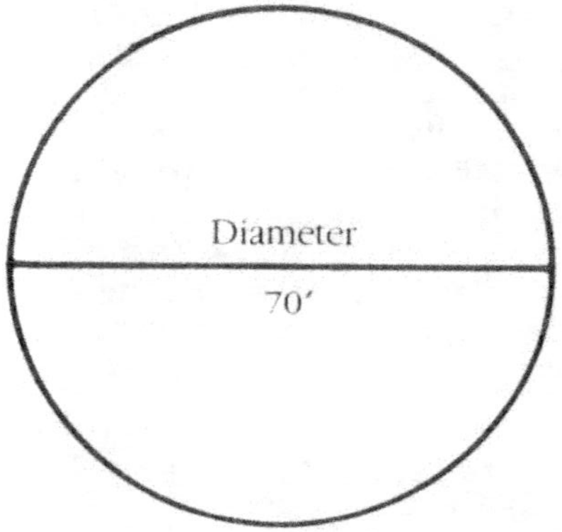

Area = 0.8 × 70′ × 70′
Area = 3,920 square feet

Area of a Right Triangle

Area = 0.5 BH
B = base
H = height

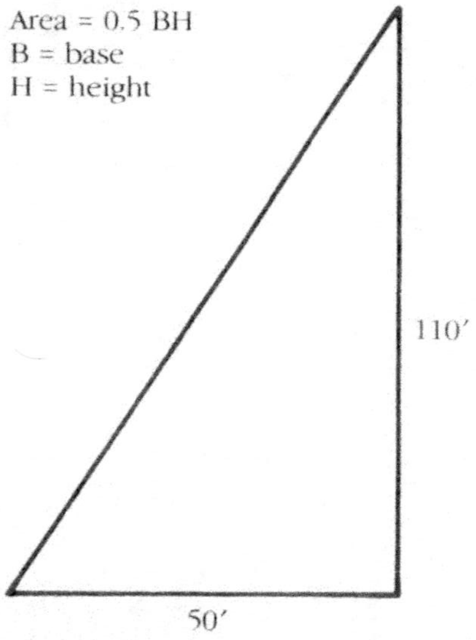

Area = 0.5 × 50′ × 110′
Area = 2,750 square feet

Area of Irregular Shape

When the lawn area is irregularly shaped, fit the area to standard geometric shapes, determine the area of all components, and add to obtain the total area.

In this example the upper section can be divided into two right triangles and the lower section into two circles. Find the individual areas of 1, 2, 3, and 4; then add all areas to determine the total.

If you know the dimensions of your property, subtract the area of the house, garage, driveway, and plantings to approximate the lawn area.

The amount of fertilizer needed to cover your lawn is determined by the total lawn area and the fertilizer rate and analysis. Review the following example:

Your established lawn is 5,000 square feet; an application of 1 pound of nitrogen per 1,000 square feet is to be applied, and you have selected a fertilizer with the analysis 25-5-10. Refer to table 4 on page 14 to find the amount of fertilizer to apply to provide 1 pound of nitrogen per 1,000 square feet. You will find that 4 pounds of 25-5-10 will be needed to provide 1 pound of nitrogen per 1,000 square feet.

4 lb 25-5-10 × .25 = 1 lb total nitrogen
4 lb 25-5-10 × .05 = 0.2 lb phosphate
4 lb 25-5-10 × .10 = 0.4 lb potash

To cover the entire lawn area of 5,000 square feet, you will need 20 pounds of this particular fertilizer, i.e., 4 pounds/1,000 square feet times 5,000 square feet equals 20 pounds of 25-5-10 for 5,000 square feet.

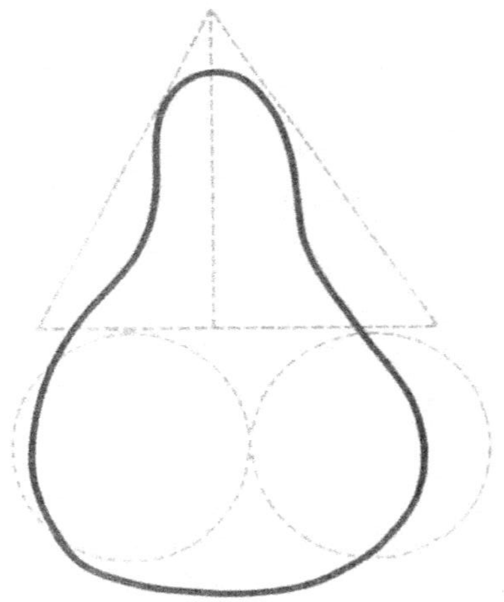

Directions for Sampling Soils

Routine soil sampling is the best way to determine the soil nutrient levels and the pH level. This is the only way to know the proper fertilizer type and rate to apply to maintain a healthy, vigorous lawn.

Timing

The best time to sample the soil is before a lawn is established. Proper soil amendments can then be purchased and incorporated into the seedbed before seeding or sodding.

It is advisable to have your soil tested every other year unless there has been a history of soil-related problems. Samples can be taken any time during the year when the soil is not frozen. Always sample the soil at the same time each year so that comparisons can be made. The two preferred times to sample the soil are early spring, so that results can be received well in advance to plan for the upcoming growing season, and fall, to plan for the next year's growing season.

Do not take a soil sample from an area that has had lime or fertilizer applied recently, within 3–4 weeks.

LAWN DISEASES

How to Control Them

CONTENTS

	Page
Fungus Diseases	
Helminthosporium leafspot and foot rot	1
Brown patch	2
Rust	3
Pythium diseases	3
Dollar spot	4
Stripe smut	4
Powdery mildew	5
Fusarium blight	6
Red thread	6
Copper spot	7
Ophiobolus patch	7
Snow molds: Fusarium patch and Typhula blight	8
Mushrooms and fairy rings	9
Slime molds	9
Other Causes of Poor Turf	10
Undesirable species	10
Undesirable mixtures	10
Insect injury	10
Fertilizer burn	10
Hydrated lime burn	10
Pesticide injury	10
Dog urine injury	10
Improper mowing	10
Improper watering	10
Buried debris	11
Accumulation of runners	11
Compacted soils	11

LAWN DISEASES

How to Control Them

Most of the grasses in lawns grow under artificial conditions and are more subject to attack by disease organisms than they would be in a natural environment. Healthy, vigorously growing, adapted lawn grasses that are properly managed can best survive disease attacks.

The homeowner's best defense against lawn diseases is to follow these basic principles of lawn establishment and maintenance:

- Select grasses adapted to the soil, climatic, and light conditions under which they will be grown.
- Spend the necessary time, effort, and money on caring for the lawn. In addition to disease control, lawn care includes proper fertilizing, watering, mowing, and insect and weeds control.

Proper care does not completely prevent or cure diseases, but it helps to curb them so that chemical controls can be more effective if they become necessary.

Knowing how to diagnose the most common causes of dead or injured grass and knowing the recommended treatments for various unhealthy conditions will help the homeowner to prevent serious lawn damage. Poor turf may be due to disease or to any one or a combination of other causes—undesirable or un adapted species, insect damage, fertilizer and chemical burning, dog urine, improper mowing, improper watering, localized dry spots, and compacted soil.

FUNGUS DISEASES

Fungi cause most of the serious and widespread diseases of lawn grasses. All the diseases discussed in this section are fungus diseases. Most of the fungi that attack lawn grasses occur in the form of microscopically small filaments, or threads. The mass of threads, which sometimes have a cobwebby appearance, are called mycelium. Many fungi reproduce by means of microscopic fruiting structures called spores.

Only those fungi that get their nutrients from a living host are true disease organisms. Such organisms cause Helminthosporium leaf spot, fading-out, brown patch, rust, grease spot, dollar spot, stripe smut, and snow mold.

Mushrooms and slime molds in lawns are examples of fungi that are not true disease organisms. They do not attack lawn grasses directly, but are discussed with disease organisms because they are a common lawn problem.

HELMINTHOSPORIUM LEAFSPOT AND FOOT ROT

This disease, which gets its name from the Helminthosporium fungi that cause it, is one of the most widely distributed and destructive grass diseases. Kentucky bluegrass is one of the species most severely damaged.

The principal fungus causing leafspot in Kentucky bluegrass also causes a foot rot condition known as going-out or melting-out. The disease occurs mainly during cool, moist weather of spring and fall, but it may develop throughout the summer. Pure stands of Kentucky bluegrass favor development of the disease; mixtures of several recommended species usually retard development, because most mixtures contain naturally resistant species.

Symptoms

Damage is most conspicuous in the leaves. However, the fungus responsible for the disease also causes a sheath rot or foot rot. The fungus produces reddish-brown to purplish-black spots on leaves and stems of Kentucky bluegrass. Leaves shrivel and the steams, crowns, rhizomes, and roots discolor and rot. Leaf spots and foot rots produced on other grasses by different species of Helminthosporium resemble those on Kentucky bluegrass. Dead grass in attacked areas often is attributed to drought injury. Weeds and crabgrass usually invade these areas.

Control

In Kentucky bluegrass lawns, you can control the disease by growing less susceptible varieties such as Fylking, Merion, Penn-star, and Windsor. Some leafspot-ting may occur, but these varieties are more resistant than ordinary Kentucky bluegrass and are seldom killed during-the destructive foot rot stage.

Follow these management practices to reduce damage: Mow upright-growing grasses to a height of 13A, to 2 inches rather than 1/2 to 1 inch. Apply enough fertilizer to keep grass healthy and thriving. Avoid overstimulation with nitrogen, particularly in the spring. Remove clippings, especially on lawns receiving heavy fertilization.

Fungicides that control *Helminthosporium* leaf spot are listed on page 12.

BROWN PATCH

The fungus responsible for brown patch attacks practically all species of grasses, but it is most serious on bentgrasses, fes-cues, Kentucky bluegrass, ryegrass, centipede grass, and St. Augustinegrass. Brown patch is one of the most prevalent lawn grass diseases in the warm, humid regions of the United States. It occurs during warm, wet weather. Brown patch is most damaging following excessive applications of nitrogen fertilizer. This promotes a lush growth of grass that is readily attacked. The disease spreads by fungus threads, or mycelium. New infections can start from mycelium carried on shoes, mowing equipment, or grass clippings.

Symptoms

Brown patch is characterized by development of irregular circular areas a few inches to several feet in diameter with a brownish discoloration. In bentgrasses a narrow, dark, smoke-colored ring borders the diseased area. This disappears when the weather becomes cool or dry. Sometimes only the leaves are affected and the turf recovers in 2 or 3 weeks. However, if the disease is severe and weather conditions remain favorable for its development, it attacks the crowns and kills the grass. The dead grass generally remains erect and does not lie flat like grass killed by grease spot, a *Pythium* disease. The fungus threads, or mycelium, are frequently observed as filmy, white tufts early in the morning while the grass is still wet with dew. As the leaves dry, the fungus threads shrivel and disappear, and only dead and dying leaves are left. After several weeks, new grass grows back into the affected area.

Control

Management practices that help in control: Avoid excessive applications of nitrogen fertilizer. Water lawns early in the day to give grass leaves time to dry out before night. Remove clippings if excessive.

Brown patch can be controlled if the lawn is watered 48 hours before treating with fungicide and if this is repeated three times at weekly intervals.

RUST

Rust fungi attack many lawn grasses. Rust usually occurs in late summer and remains until frost. Heavy dew favors its development.

Rust damage is more severe on Merion Kentucky bluegrass and zoysia than on other grasses. Meyer and Emerald zoysias are susceptible to rust infection.

Rust has appeared on Merion Kentucky bluegrass from Rhode Island to California and from Canada to Oklahoma. The rust fungus seems to attack Merion wherever it is grown.

Some Kentucky bluegrass varieties resist rust infection entirely. Common Kentucky bluegrass is less susceptible to rust than Merion. However, it is vulnerable to the more destructive *Helminthosporium* leaf spot.

Symptoms

Symptoms are yellow-orange or red-brown powdery pustules that develop on leaves and stems. If a cloth is rubbed across affected leaves, the rust-colored spores adhere to the cloth and produce a yellowish or orange stain.

Control

Lawns containing pure stands of Merion Kentucky bluegrass are especially susceptible to attack by rust fungi. Damage is less severe if Merion Kentucky bluegrass is mixed with common Kentucky bluegrass or with red fescue. Recommended mixtures are 50-percent Merion and 50-percent common Kentucky bluegrass ; 50-percent Merion Kentucky bluegrass and 50-percent red fescue; or 50-percent Merion, 25-percent common Kentucky bluegrass, and 25-percent red fescue.

The Kentucky bluegrass varieties, Fylking, Pennstar, and Kenblue are more rust-resistant than Merion.

Mowing, fertilizing, and watering practices recommended in the summary of management practices (page 16) will help control rust.

Several chemicals (see p. 13) control rust on Merion Kentucky bluegrass and other grasses. Chemicals do not completely eradicate rust or prevent infection of growth that comes out after treatment. Repeated applications may be necessary to keep rust under control, especially on Merion Kentucky bluegrass.

PYTHIUM DISEASES

The two most destructive lawn diseases caused by Pythium fungi are grease spot and cottony blight. Grease spot occurs in many parts of the country on a wide range of grasses; cottony blight occurs mainly on ryegrass in the South.

Pythium diseases occur in humid areas and may be more widespread than is generally realized. The fungi are destructive at 70° F, and above, especially in poorly drained soils. These diseases are most common on newly established turf, but if conditions are favorable they occur on grass regardless of age.

Symptoms

Diseased areas vary from a few inches to several feet in diameter and they sometimes occur in streaks as though the fungus had spread from mowing or from water flow following heavy rains. Injury is most noticeable in early morning as a circular spot or group of spots about 2 inches in diameter surrounded by blackened grass blades that are intertwined with the fungus threads. Diseased leaves become water soaked, mat together, and appear slimy. The darkened grass blades soon wither and become reddish brown, particularly if the weather is sunny and windy. Grass is usually killed in 24 hours and it lies flat on the ground rather than remaining upright like grass affected by the brown patch disease. New grass does not grow back into the diseased area.

Control

The most important management recommendation is to avoid watering methods that keep foliage and ground wet for long periods. Other suggestions: Avoid excessive watering during warm weather. Delay seeding until fall because cool, dry weather generally checks the disease.

Chemicals give best results if used when the disease first appears (see page.12).

DOLLAR SPOT

Dollar spot, also known as small brown patch, occurs on many species of grasses. The disease is particularly destructive in bentgrass-es. It is most prevalent in the humid northern areas of the United States but occurs also in States farther south.

The fungus is most destructive during cool, wet weather. It generally attacks in May and June, stops during July and August, and starts again in September and October. Dollar spot may occur in any turf regardless of management or soil fertility, but damage usually is greatest if there is a deficiency of nitrogen.

Symptoms

The disease is characterized by development of bleached spots the size of a silver dollar. Affected grass is killed, and the turf is left pitted. Sometimes the diseased areas merge and form large, irregular patches. At first, spots of diseased grass are dark and somewhat water soaked; then they turn brown and ultimately bleach nearly white. If the fungus is growing actively, a fine, white, cobwebby mycelium can be seen when dew is still on the grass. Sometimes only the uppermost grass blades are affected and light colored blotches develop on them.

Turf recovers quickly if treated with fungicides in the early stages of a disease attack; if left untreated it may take many weeks for new grass to fill in dead areas.

The best control is to use chemicals listed on page 13.

STRIPE SMUT

Stripe smut fungus attacks several lawn grasses but it is most prevalent and destructive on Merion Kentucky bluegrass, principally in the northern half of the United States.

Smut spores in contaminated soil germinate and produce infection threads that invade grass seedlings and young tillers. Since the fungus grows systematically, infected plants remain diseased until they die.

Symptoms

Narrow gray or black stripes that may be continuous or discontinuous develop lengthwise in leaf blades. The gray stripes are unruptured smut sites called sori. The black streaks result when smut sori rupture and liberate a mass of black, powdery spores. Following rupture of the sori, diseased leaves wither, curl, and shred from the tip downward, and die.

Diseased Kentucky bluegrass plants occur singly, or in spots from a few inches to a foot or more in diameter. Infected plants are often pale green to slightly yellowed. They also are shorter than neighboring healthy plants and may be obscured by them.

Stripe smut is most readily seen on leaves during cool weather in spring and fall. Diseased plants are difficult to find during hot, dry weather because many infected plants die. Smutted plants also are difficult to find shortly after mowing due to their slower growth.

Control

Fungicides are available for treating the disease. Smut damage is less severe if Merion Kentucky bluegrass is mixed with common Kentucky bluegrass, or if smut-tolerant varieties like Fylking, Kenblue, Park, or Pennstar are grown

POWDERY MILDEW

In recent years, powdery mildew has become an increasingly important fungus disease of Mer-ion Kentucky bluegrass and other Kentucky bluegrasses. Powdery mildew also infects red fescue, bermuda, and other grasses used for lawns. The use of high rates of nitrogen fertilizer produces an ideal environment for this mildew fungus.

The disease is generally more damaging to grasses in shaded and protected areas (on north and east sides of buildings), although it also occurs in severe form in fields of Merion during late fall and early spring. Because the fungus significantly reduces the growth of leaves, roots, and rhizomes, it is an important cause of turf deterioration of bluegrass lawns in shaded areas. Many plants may be weakened, die from drought, or be winter-killed because of this deterioration.

Symptoms

Powdery mildew appears first as small superficial patches of white to light-gray fungus growth on leaves and sheaths. These patches enlarge rapidly and become powdery as spores are produced. The older, lower leaves are often completely covered by mildew. The leaf tissue under the mildew becomes yellowed soon after infection and later turns tan or brown and is killed. Severely infected leaves gradually dry up and die.

The fungus survives the winter as a mass of thread-like filaments on the live leaves of Kentucky bluegrass. Numerous spores are produced on these filaments in the spring. Spores are carried by the wind and initiate new infections during cool (optimum 65° F.), humid weather. With favorable temperature and high atmospheric humidity, the host tissue dies and the spores are carried to other grasses in the same or neighboring turf areas to produce new infections and start the cycle once again.

Control

Kentucky bluegrass varieties differ in their susceptibility to powdery mildew. Merion is very susceptible while other varieties exhibit varying degrees of resistance.

To reduce turf shading and improve air circulation be sure to prune or remove trees and shrubs that shade or border turf areas. Keep the lawn vigorous but avoid overstimulation with nitrogen fertilizer. Water during dry periods to maintain adequate moisture in the soil. Where possible, mow at the recommended height and—when the disease is present—collect all clippings.

In the spring or early fall, when powdery mildew becomes evident, one or more applications of a fungicide at 7 to 10 day intervals should control the disease. Suggested fungicides to obtain control are listed in the guide on page 12.

FUSARIUM BLIGHT

Fusarium blight affects Kentucky bluegrass, bentgrass, red fescue, and many other grasses. The fungi that cause Fusarium blight survive the winter months in infected grass roots, crowns, and in thatch covering the lower portion of grass plants. The pathogens are widespread; they occur on blighted turf wherever the above turf grasses are grown.

Bentgrasses are the most susceptible species, followed by Kentucky bluegrass and red fescue. The disease also occurs in Merion and Windsor Kentucky bluegrass, other varieties vary in susceptibility at different temperatures.

The severity of the disease varies directly with light intensity; areas that receive direct sunlight are the most severely infected. Infection of the leaves usually occurs when air temperatures are 70° F. to 90° F. and conditions of high humidity prevail. The disease ceases to be active when temperatures fall below 70° F. and there is an absence of rainfall or humidity.

Symptoms

At first, diseased areas are light green but within 36 to 48 hours the areas fade to tan and then to a light straw color. The diseased areas vary in size from a few inches to 2 or more feet in diameter. Dead areas may be circular, crescent shaped, streaked, or in circles with a patch of green grass in the central portion. The latter forms a distinctive "frog's eye" symptom pattern. Extensive damage occurs when diseased areas are numerous and coalesce.

Individual plants are killed when the crown tissues are destroyed. On individual leaves, the disease is characterized by irregular-shaped, dark-green blotches. These blotches rapidly fade to a light green, then assume a reddish-brown hue, and finally become dull tan.

Control

The fungi that cause Fusarium blight grow in a layer of thatch on the soil surface. To control this disease, remove most of the thatch layer with a rake or lawnmower. A nitrogen imbalance in the soil causes the thatch on which the fungi feed to accumulate more rapidly.

To effectively control Fusarium blight the use of a preventive fungicide spray as well as thatch control is essential. Do not spray when night temperatures fall below 70° F. Spraying should be continued at 7-to-10 day intervals as long as daytime temperatures are 75° F. and above and conditions of high humidity prevail.

Fungicides that will help control Fusarium blight are listed on page 12.

RED THREAD

Red thread especially affects bentgrasses, red fescue, and Kentucky bluegrasses in the Northeastern States and in the Pacific Coast States of Washington and Oregon. In these regions, red thread occurs primarily in the early spring and fall during cool, wet weather. This fungus disease has also been reported on Bermuda-grass lawns in Mississippi during December.

When the grass is growing rapidly, nitrogen fertilization is a rapid and effective means of controlling the disease. However, the fungus again becomes destructive when grass growth slows down. Therefore, fungicidal eradication is necessary for satisfactory disease control.

The pathogen survives unfavorable conditions as fragments of dried fungal tissues and as dormant mycelium in the residues of the diseased plants. These fragments may be carried by the wind or mechanically on mowers or similar machines.

Symptoms

The fungus attacks the leaves and leaf sheaths. These parts later become tan colored as the tissue dries out. The leaves may be completely covered by a pink, gelatinous growth of the fungus. As this growth spreads, it infects plant after plant.

In its final stages, the disease is characterized by reddish fungus threads at the leaf terminals. Diseased areas are usually 2 to 30 inches in diameter and irregular in shape.

Red thread is capable of growing over a wide range of temperatures; growth occurs from slightly above 32° F. to about 86° F. The most favorable temperature range for growth lies between 60° F. and 70° F.

Control

Red thread is serious only when cool temperatures slow grass growth or when the turf is under-fertilized with nitrogen. Fungicides to control red thread are listed on page 12.

COPPER SPOT

Copper spot can cause a serious disease problem on bentgrasses. It is most damaging in the coastal states but is found throughout the United States.

The pathogen overwinters in the debris of the previous season's growth. The disease occurs in warm, wet weather; active growth of the organism begins when air temperatures range from 68° F. to 75° F. When the weather is warm and humid secondary spores are produced and new lesions are formed.

The spores, spread by means of splashing water, germinate rapidly and new leaf infections take place within 24 hours. Outbreaks of copper spot may occur in epidemic proportions within a few days.

Symptoms

From a distance, copper spot looks like salmon-pink or copper-colored turf; the spots range from 1 to 3 inches in diameter. Unlike areas infected by dollar spot, areas affected by copper spot are not definite in outline. Wet weather increases the intensity of coloration.

Control

Copper spot can be controlled by the use of fungicides. Apply preventive fungicidal applications at 10-day intervals when the daytime air temperatures stabilize at 70° F. to 75° F. Make curative applications at 4 to 5-day intervals until recovery is effected.

Fungicides that will control copper spot are listed on page 16.

OPHIOBOLUS PATCH

Ophiobolus patch is the third most important fungus disease in the Pacific Northwest. It occurs west of the Cascades in Oregon, Washington, and British Columbia. The disease is especially common on bentgrass lawns.

The growth of the disease is stimulated by cool, wet weather. However, symptoms become most noticeable during midsummer under drier growing conditions. The disease usually appears as a thinning or drying of the grass in doughtnut-shaped rings or larger areas. Both shoots and roots of the grass are severely attacked. Affected areas do not recover for several months.

Symptoms

The doughtnut-shaped rings range from several inches to several feet in diameter. The injured areas are light brown in color becoming dull gray in winter. The centers of the rings are invaded by weeds and annual bluegrass.

Ophiobolus patch is first seen as depressed circular patches of blighted turfgrass, a few inches in diameter. The affected areas may increase to several feet in diameter and coalesce so that they become large, irregular-shaped patches. The colors range from light straw to bronze. The centers of the patches often fill in with resistant species creating a "frog' eye" symptom pattern.

Control

Ophiobolus patch is difficult to control with fungicides. The use of ammonium sulfate fertilizer as a source of nitrogen has been effective.

Apply ammonium sulfate four times a year in March, May, June, and early September. Apply 7? pounds of the product as it comes from the bag per 1,000 square feet for each application. Turf must be thoroughly watered after each application of fertilizer.

To balance applications of ammonium sulfate apply 0-20-20 (O-P-K) fertilizer twice a year in early spring and early fall. Use 7 pounds of fertilizer per 1,000 square feet for each application. After the disease has disappeared use a 12-4-8 fertilizer for normal lawn fertilization.

SNOW MOLDS: FUSARIUM PATCH AND TYPHULA BLIGHT

These diseases are especially severe on bentgrasses, but they also occur on other lawn grasses. Snow mold, or winter scald, is caused by several different fungi. It is most severe when snow covers grass for long periods. It is particularly difficult to control if the grass is green and growing actively when covered by lasting snow. Fusarium patch, also known as pink snow mold, can occur during the growing season when humidity is high and daily temperatures fall below 65°F. Any condition that keeps the turf excessively wet, such as poor surface drainage, favors these diseases.

Symptoms

Snow mold symptoms appear first as a white cottony growth on the leaves. As the leaves die they turn light brown and cling together. Diseased areas are usually 1 to 12 inches or more in diameter and discolored dirty white, gray, or slightly pink. Fusarium patch is characterized by development of irregular pale yellow areas from several inches to several feet in diameter. Later, affected areas become whitish gray. Sometimes the edge of an affected area has a faint pinkish color.

Typhula blight is particularly active under snow cover and is usually conspicuous at the first spring thaw. At first, the disease appears as light-yellow discolored grass areas 1 or 2 inches in diameter. Leaves of the infected plants change their discolored appearance to a grayish white. As the areas enlarge, a halo of grayish-white mycelial growth up to 1 inch in diameter develops. Affected areas may measure up to 1 or 2 feet, but under optimum conditions the diseased grass may coalesce into larger areas.

Initial disease development does not occur unless there is snow cover on unfrozen ground. When the ground is frozen, parasitic activity of the fungus essentially ceases. The disease is most active with the advent of cool air temperatures and humid conditions in the spring.

Control

Proper management in the fall is especially important because the condition of the turf as it goes into the winter determines whether the snow mold fungus can easily get established. Do not apply high nitrogen fertilizers late in the fall because that might stimulate growth and result in an actively growing turf when snow covers the ground. Keep the lawn cut in the fall to prevent a mat of grass from developing. Apply lime if soil tests indicate a need for it.

For control of snow molds with fungicides, see table on page 17.

MUSHROOMS AND FAIRY RINGS

Many kinds of mushrooms grow in lawns and turf areas. They vary in size, shape, and habit of growth, and in the way they affect the turf. They may grow individually or in clumps. Some grow in a circle and cause a condition known as fairy rings.

Mushrooms

Mushrooms that grow individually or in clumps usually develop from buried organic matter such as pieces of construction lumber, logs, or tree stumps. Mushrooms with this growth habit are usually harmless to grasses but are objectionable because they are un sightly and the fruiting bodies occur repeatedly. They develop following prolonged wet weather, and often disappear as soon as the soil begins to dry or when the grass is mowed.

Eliminate mushrooms that grow from buried lumber, logs, or stumps by digging up the pieces of buried wood. If this is impractical, drench the soil with captan. The simplest way to drench is to punch holes 6 to 8 inches apart and 6 to 8 inches deep in the ground within and surrounding the, infected area. Use an iron rod or pipe for punching the holes, and then pour a solution of captan down the holes.

Fairy Rings

Fairy rings are circles, or arcs, of dark-green grass surrounding areas of light-colored or dead grass. During spring and fall the fruiting bodies (mushrooms) develop in a circle outlining the fairy ring. Unless the fungus is controlled the ring enlarges each year and leaves alternate bands of green and discolored grass.

The fungus that causes fairy rings begins growth at a particular point and continues to grow outward. It may spread from 5 to 24 inches annually; the rate of spread depends on soil conditions, temperature, moisture, and fertility. The fungus is usually several inches below the ground and it forms a dense layer of mycelial threads that break down organic matter at the outer edge of the ring. Grass at the outer edge grows faster than grass outside the ring, and is darker green. Dying or dead grass is inside the zone of stimulated growth. Fairy rings seldom occur in lawns that are adequately fertilized and treated with fungicides for control of other diseases.

For best control, fumigate the affected area with methyl bromide. As an alternate method, punch holes around the outside of the ring and throughout the affected area, then pour a solution of captan into the holes.

SLIME MOLDS

A group of fungi known as slime molds often covers grass with a dusty, bluish-gray, black, or yellow mass. Slime molds are not parasitic on grass, but they are unsightly. They feed on dead organic matter. The most damage they do to grass plants is to shade and discolor the blades. Slime molds occur during wet weather; they disappear rapidly as soon as it becomes dry. The large masses can be readily broken up by sweeping with a broom or by spraying with a strong stream of water. During prolonged damp weather slime molds can be especially annoying and it may be desirable to apply a turf fungicide listed on 13 to affected areas.

OTHER CAUSES OF POOR TURF

UNDESIRABLE SPECIES

Short-lived perennials like red-top and ryegrass or weedy annuals such as annual bluegrass and crabgrass do not make a desirable lawn. Annual species usually die at the end of the growing season, and leave brown or bare areas that may be mistaken for disease injury.

UNDESIRABLE MIXTURES

Bermudagrasses and zoysia-grasses turn straw colored or brown following a killing frost. When these species are grown in a sod composed mainly of cool-season grasses, a mottled brown and green lawn often results because of the differences in sensitivity to cold. This effect may resemble disease injury.

INSECT INJURY

Lawn grasses are often damaged by insect pests. For information concerning lawn insects and their control, see your county agent or write to the U.S. Department of Agriculture, Washington, D.C. 20250.

FERTILIZER BURN

Concentrated inorganic fertilizers, if applied too heavily, burn grass in 2 or 3 days. Burned areas may occur in spots or streaks or the entire lawn may be damaged. To prevent injury, apply the fertilizer evenly in recommended amounts when the grass is dry,
then water immediately. If burning occurs, water generously to wash off excess fertilizer and reduce injury.

HYDRATED LIME BURN

Hydrated lime burns grass if it is applied unevenly and in large amounts. Ground agricultural limestone is safer and is usually recommended for lawns.

PESTICIDE INJURY

Some of the chemicals used for disease, insect, and weed control are potent and may injure grass if improperly applied. Chemical formulations vary with manufacturers. Follow directions and observe all precautions on the label.

DOG URINE INJURY

This kind of injury is frequently mistaken for disease damage. Affected spots are usually round or slightly irregular and variable in size. The grass within the spot turns brown or straw colored and usually dies.

IMPROPER MOWING

Cutting grass too closely or too frequently may result in a condition that looks like disease. Cut Kentucky bluegrass, red fescue, and other grasses with upright growth habit to a height of 13%, to 2 inches. Do not lower the height of cutting in midseason; it may result in serious injury. Mow the grass before it gets too talk; not more than one-half of the leaf surfaces should be removed at one time. The frequency of mowing will depend on quantity of fertilizer and water applied, weather conditions, and other factors that influence plant growth. Clippings need not be removed unless growth is excessive.

IMPROPER WATERING

Frequent light watering induces shallow rooting in grasses. Shallowrooted grasses are readily injured during periods of severe drought. Frequent evening watering favors disease development because it keeps grass leaves moist for long periods.

Do not water grass until it begins to wilt, and then apply enough water to soak the soil to a depth of 6 inches or more. It is more economical to water the lawn only when water is needed and it is better for the grass.

BURIED DEBRIS

A thin layer of soil over rocks or debris such as lumber, stumps, plaster, and cement dries rapidly and may not retain enough moisture to keep grass green. Correct this condition by removing the cause.

ACCUMULATION OF RUNNERS

Another type of dry spot results when an accumulation of runners (thatch) in bermuda-grass, bentgrass, and zoysiagrass becomes impervious and does not let water into the soil. Mowing following vigorous hand raking corrects this condition.

COMPACTED SOILS

Saturated soils pack easily and bake hard when dry, especially where traffic is heavy. The soil may become packed so hard that water will not penetrate the surface. Grass then thins out and bare spots result. To correct this condition, loosen or perforate the soil with a tined fork or aerifying implement and, if necessary, fertilize and reseed the lawn.

COMPONENTS OF RECOMMENDED FUNGICIDES

Acti-dione TGF: ® 3- [2-(3,5-dimethy1-2-oxocyclohexyl) 2 - hydroxyethyl] glutarimide (cycloheximide)

Acti-dione-thiram: cyloheximide plus bis(dimethylthiocarbamoyl) disulfide
Captan: *N*- [(trichloromethyl) thio] - 4-cyclohexene -1,2-dicar-boximide

Cleary 3336: ® diethyl [(1, 2-phenylene) bis (iminocarbonothioyl)] bis [carbamate] (thiophanate)

Daconil 2787: ® tetrachloroiso-phthalonitrile (chlorothalonil)

Dexon: ® sodium *p*-(dimethylamino) benzenediazosulfonate

Dowfume MC-2: ® methyl bromide with 2% chloropicrin
Dyrene: ® 2, 4-dichloro-6-(*o*-chioroanilino) -*s*-triazine

Fore ® coordination product of zinc ion and manganous ethylenebis [dithiocarbamate]
Fungo 50: ® dimethyl [(1,2-phenylene) bis (iminocarbonothioyl) bis [carbamate] (thiophanate-methyl)

Koban: ® 5-ethoxy-3-(trichloro-methyl)-1,2,4-thiadiazole

Mertect 140-F: ® 2- (4-thiazolyl) benzimidazole (thiabendazole)

Tersan 1991: ® methyl 1-(butylcarbamoyl) - 2 - benzimidazolecarbamate (benomyl)

Tersan LSR: ® manganous ethylenebis [dithiocarbamate] (maneb)

Tersan SP: ® 1,4-dichloro-2,5-dimethoxybenzene (chioroneb)
Zineb: zinc ethylenebis [dithiocarbamate]
® denotes a trademark or proprietary product

GUIDE FOR SELECTING FUNGICIDES

Disease and Causal Organism	Fungicides [1]	Application Per 1,000 sq ft: Ounces of Formulation	Application Per 1,000 sq ft: Tablespoons	Directions [2]
Brown Patch	Cleary's 3336® WP 50%	2	11	Disease can appear from June to August. Treat your lawn every 5–10 days until the disease has been controlled.
Rhizoctonia solani	Daconil 2787® WP 75%	4	22	
	Dyrene® WP 50%	4–6	19–28	
	Fore® WP 80%	4	14	
	Fungo 50® WP 50%	2	11	
	Mertect 140–F® liquid	2	4	
	Tersan 1991® WP 50%	2	11	
	Tersan LSR® WP 80%	6	4–5	
Copper Spot *Gloeocercospora sorghi*	See Dollar Spot (Sclerotinia)			
Dollar Spot	Acti-dione-Thiram® WP	2–4	11–22	Disease can appear from June to October. Treat your lawn at 7–14 day intervals until the disease has been controlled.
Sclerotinia	Cleary's 3336® WP 50%	2	11	
homeocarpa	Daconil 2787® WP 75%	2–4	11–22	
	Dyrene® WP 50%	4–6	19–28	
	Tersan 1991® WP 50%	2	11	
	Fore® WP 80%	6–8	14–21	
	Fungo 50® WP 50%	1	6	
	Mertect 140–F® liquid	2	4	
Fairy Rings	Captan WP 50%	4–5	15–20	Disease can appear throughout the growing season. Pour double or triple strength concentrate of captan into 1-inch holes punched 4–6 inches deep and 6–8 inches apart both inside and outside the affected area. Alternative method: Fumigate infected area with Dowfume MC–2® (1 lb/100 sq ft) and reseed or resod. Recommended largely for golf courses, parks, and other large turf areas.
Mushrooms	Dowfume MC–2			
Psalliota campestris				
Marasmius				
Lepiota				
Fusarium Blight	Cleary's 3336® WP 50%	2–4	11–22	Treat at first appearance of disease and repeat 10–14 days later. Water thoroughly to wet into soil.
Fusarium roseum	Fungo 50® WP 50%	4–8	19–38	
	Tersan 1991® WP 50%	2	33	
Grease Spot and	Tersan SP® WP 65%	4	5–6	Disease can appear from July to September and in fall and winter during warm, humid periods in the South. Treat your lawn every 5–14 days until the disease has been controlled.
Cottony Blight	Dexon® WP 70%	2	14	
Pythium	Fore® WP 80%	8	28	
	Koban® WP 65%	4	17	
	Zineb WP 75%	2	13–27	
Helminthosporium diseases	Acti-dione-Thiram® WP	4	22	Disease can appear from April to August depending on kind of grass and species of fungus. Treat your lawn every 7–14 days three times consecutively or until the disease has been controlled.
Leafspot (Blight,	Captan WP 50%	4–6	15–23	
Going-out,	Cleary's 3336® WP 50%	2	11	
Melting-out)	Daconil 2787 ® WP 75%	4	22	
Helminthosporium	Dyrene® WP 50%	4–6	19–28	
spp.	Fore® WP 80%	4	14	
	Tersan LSR® WP 80%	3–4	4–5	
	Zineb WP 75%	2	13–27	
Ophiobolus Patch *Ophiobolus graminis*	See page — for control.			
Powdery Mildew	Acti-dione Thiram®	4	22	July–September
Erysiphe graminis	Acti-dione TGF® WP	1–2	6	7–10 days
	Tersan 1991® WP 50%	2	11	7–14 days
Red Thread	Acti-dione-Thiram® WP	4	22	May, June, and August, every 10–14 days.
Corticum fuciforme	Cleary's 3336® WP 50%	2	11	
	Fore® WP 80%	4–6	14–21	
	Fungo 50® WP 50%	2	11	
	Tersan LSR® WP 80%	6	4–5	

GUIDE FOR SELECTING FUNGICIDES—continued

Disease and Causal Organism	Fungicides [1]	Application Per 1,000 sq ft: Ounces of Formulation	Application Per 1,000 sq ft: Tablespoons	Directions [2]
Rust *Puccinia*	Acti-dione-Thiram® WP	4	22	Disease can appear from June to September. Treat your lawn every 7–14 days until rust disappears.
	Daconil 2787® WP 75%	4	22	
	Dyrene® WP 50%	4–6	19–28	
	Fore® WP 80%	4	14	
	Tersan LSR® WP 80%	3–4	4–5	
	Zineb WP 75%	2	13–27	
lime Molds *Physarum cinercum*	Fore® WP 80%	6–8	21–28	Disease can appear throughout the growing season and can be controlled without fungicides. See page —.
	Zineb WP 75%	2	13–27	
now Molds Fusarium Patch *Fusarium nivale*	Tersan 1991® WP 50%	2	11	Disease can appear from fall to spring. Treat your law at intervals of 2–6 weeks as needed.
	Mertect 140–F® liquid	2	2	
	Fore® WP 80%	6–8	21–28	
	Fungo 50® WP 50%	2	11	
Typhula Blight *Typhula itoana*	Tersan SP® WP 65%	6–8	5–6	Disease can appear from fall to spring. Tret your lawn at intervals of 2–6 weeks as needed.
	Dyrene WP 50%	2–3	19–28	
Stripe Smut *Ustilago striiformis*	Fungo 50® WP 50%	4–8	19–38	One application in October or early spring before grass growth begins. Water thoroughly to wet into soil.
	Tersan 1991® WP 50%	6	33	

CAUTION: Do not graze treated areas or feed clippings to livestock.

[1] See page 17 for components of registered fungicides.

[2] The directions given in the above table may not be complete enough. Be sure to read and follow the manufacturer's directions on the label for all fungicide applications.

MANAGEMENT PRACTICES THAT HELP PREVENT LAWN DISEASES

These practices are general guides to be used according to one's judgment. Their importance depends on the kind and seriousness of the disease threat. Not all of them are practicable under all conditions.

- Select grass species best adapted to the soil, climatic, and light Conditions under which they will be grown.
- Plant mixtures of recommended grasses. Species vary in their susceptibility to different disease organisms, and in a mixture one or more of the grasses usually will survive a severe disease attack.
- Do not clip upright-growing grasses such as Kentucky bluegrass and red fescue too closely-1 ¾ to 2 inches is the best height. Creeping grasses such as bent-grass and zoysia may be clipped at ½ inch or less.
- Mow the grass before it gets too tall ; not more than one-half of the leaf surface should be removed at one time.
- Mow the lawn frequently enough in the fall to prevent the accumulation of a thick mat of grass before snow comes.
- Apply enough fertilizer to keep grass vigorously growing, but• avoid over stimulating the grass with nitrogen. Apply lime if soil tests indicate a need for it.
- Clippings need not be removed except on heavily fertilized lawns or during periods when the grass is growing rapidly. Clippings provide nutrients for fungi and help to maintain humidity long after the sun has dried off surrounding uncovered areas.
- Water early enough in the day to allow grass leaves time to dry out before night. Avoid frequent, light watering, especially during warm weather.
- Do not water grass until it begins to wilt, then soak the soil to a depth of 6 inches or more. Provide good surface drainage.

USE OF PESTICIDES

This publication is intended for nationwide distribution. Pesticides are registered by the Environmental Protection Agency (EPA) for countrywide use unless otherwise indicated on the label.

The use of pesticides is governed by the provisions of the Federal Insecticide, Fungicide, and Rodenticide Act, as amended. This Act is administered by EPA. According to the provisions of the Act, "It shall be unlawful for any person to use any registered pesticide in a manner inconsistent with its labeling." (Section 12 (a) (2) (G))

EPA has interpreted this Section of the Act to require that the intended use of the pesticide must be on the label of the pesticide being used or covered by a Pesticide Enforcement. Policy Statement (PEPS) issued by EPA.

The optimum use of pesticides, both as to rate and frequency, may vary in different sections of the country. Users of this publication may also wish to consult their Cooperative Extension Service, State Agricultural Experiment Stations, or County Extension Agents for information applicable to their localities.

The pesticides mentioned in this publication are available in several different formulations that contain varying amounts of active ingredient. Because of this difference, the rates given in this publication refer to the amount of active ingredient, unless otherwise indicated. Users are reminded to convert the rate in the publication to the strength of the pesticide actually being used. For example, 1 pound of active ingredient equals 2 pounds of a 50 percent formulation.

The user is cautioned to read and follow all directions and precautions given on the label of the pesticide formulation being used.

Federal and State regulations require registration numbers on all pesticide containers. Use only pesticides that carry one of these registration numbers.

USDA publications that contain suggestions for the use of pesticides are normally revised at 2-year intervals. If your copy is more than 2 years old, contact your Cooperative Extension Service to determine the latest pesticide recommendations.

The pesticides mentioned in this publication were federally registered for the use indicated as of this publication. The user is cautioned to determine the directions on the label or labeling prior to use of the pesticide.

www.ingramcontent.com/pod-product-compliance
Lightning Source LLC
Chambersburg PA
CBHW082210300426
44117CB00016B/2748